JUL X X 2015

SMALL GREEN ROOFS

SMALL GREEN ROOFS

Low-Tech Options for Greener Living

Nigel Dunnett
Dusty Gedge
John Little
Edmund C. Snodgrass

TIMBER PRESS
Portland · London

Frontispiece: Converting a shipping container into a small building is one means of ensuring that there is enough structural support for a green roof. This building at Cove Park in Scotland is part of an artist's community. Photo by Cove Park

Thanks are offered to those who granted permission for use of materials but who are not named individually in the acknowledgments. While every reasonable effort has been made to contact copyright holders and secure permission for all materials reproduced in this work, we offer apologies for any instances in which this was not possible and for any inadvertent omissions.

Published in 2011 by Timber Press, Inc.
Second printing 2011

The Haseltine Building   2 The Quadrant
133 S.W. Second Avenue, Suite 450   135 Salusbury Road
Portland, Oregon 97204-3527   London NW6 6RJ
timberpress.com   timberpress.co.uk

Printed in China

Library of Congress Cataloging-in-Publication Data

Small green roofs: low-tech options for greener living/Nigel Dunnett . . . [et al.].—1st ed.
        p. cm.
Includes bibliographical references and index.
ISBN-13: 978-160469-059-0
1. Green roofs (Gardening) I. Dunnett, Nigel.
SB419.5.S63 2011
635.9'671—dc22   2010041465

A catalogue record for this book is also available from the British Library.

To my wife, Marta Herrero,
for her love, care, and support,
and my two boys,
Alex and Jack—this is for you

—Nigel Dunnett

To Dr. G. Kadas,
for her long-standing commitment,
research, and support
for green roofs and biodiversity

—Dusty Gedge

To my wife, Fi,
and our kids, Sam and Poppy,
for keeping me sane;
to my brother, Rob,
for going along with the idea;
and friends Dave, Paul, Andy, and Kelvin
for listening to me in the pub
every Friday night

—John Little

To Thomas Snodgrass,
farmer, inventor, and
a real "Do It Yourself" mentor

—Ed Snodgrass

CONTENTS

PROJECTS

INTRODUCTION

GREEN ROOFS have captured people's imagination the world over. In North America, Europe, China, Southeast Asia, Australia, and New Zealand green roofs have surged in popularity because they just seem right— right because of the way they look and because of the many benefits they bring to a building's users and owners, to the people who see the building, and to the wider surroundings that the building sits within. This sense of the inherent goodness of putting plants and nature back into the hard and stark environments of our towns and cities touches something deep within us. It cuts to the very heart of our well-being as individuals and of human society as a whole.

Greening a roof, however small, is therefore a profound act, full of meaning and symbolism. The act of greening a building or structure, whether it is retrofitted onto an existing structure or included as an element in the design of a new building, makes a deep statement about the way we see the world. Green roofs get under the skin. They become fascinating living and dynamic objects, and having or making a green roof can be life-changing. The pioneering and visionary Austrian artist and designer Friedensreich Hundertwasser, who created several notable buildings with expansive gardens and forests on their roofs, put it this way (quoted at www.gardenvisit.com):

> The true proportions in this world are the views to the stars and the views down to the surface of the earth. Grass and vegetation in the city should grow on all horizontal spaces—that is to say, wherever rain and snow falls vegetation should grow, on the roads and on the roofs. The horizontal is the domain of nature and wherever vegetation grows on the horizontal level man is off limits. I've worked a great deal with grass roofs, putting soil on top and having things grow, but there is something strange in this, more than ecological. It is a religious act to have soil on your roof and trees growing on top of you; the act reconciles you with nature—a very ancient wisdom.

The green roof on top of this house at Riomaggiore, Italy, fits nicely with the local landscape. It provides additional recreational space and habitat for birds and invertebrates, captures rainwater, and keeps the building cool beneath. Photo by Emilio Ancaya, Living Roofs, Inc.

Of course, for most of us who may wish to put a green roof on a garage or on a small building in the garden, this may seem very idealistic, rather far-fetched, and completely outside of the reasoning behind our decision to have a green roof structure. Maybe you want to improve an ugly view, encourage wildlife, keep a building cool in summer, or soak up excess rainfall runoff from the roof. Nevertheless, it is worth reminding yourself that what you are doing is also very powerful and a deliberate and positive act to make a difference. It is life-enhancing and will do *you* good, as a person, as well as doing good for the wider environment. Here's another quote, this time from Professor Stephen Kellert (in the spring 2009 issue of *Living Architecture Monitor*), who has popularized biophilic design, a field of environmental design that makes a direct link between the need to integrate buildings and nature:

> Some green roofs represent extraordinary insertions of living nature into the built environment, distinguished by their ecological value, experiential benefits, beauty and capacity to raise human comfort and satisfaction. On the other hand, some green roofs are almost totally focused on environmental impact objectives independent of human experience, emphasizing, for example, almost entirely such objectives as stormwater retention and enhanced insulation, with zero to little positive human contact with nature. In my opinion, the best green roof designs are ones that combine both environmental and human aesthetic objectives . . . and these will, I predict, ultimately be the most sustainable.

It is with small and domestic green roofs that we have a greater opportunity to achieve this objective than anywhere else because there will usually be a higher degree of ownership and care compared with the more familiar larger commercial and corporate green roofs. In writing this book, we hope to encourage as many people as possible to have a go at initiating, installing, constructing, and planting a green roof, whether it be in their own homes or gardens, as part of a community initiative, or at their place of work or recreation—anywhere there is an opportunity to bring nature back to a place where it had been previously banished. In so doing we, of course, wish to increase the total number of green roofs

Even the smallest of spaces are suitable for greening. Here a green roof for wildlife is installed on an apartment balcony. Photo by Dusty Gedge

that we have around us, for the benefit of all. But more than that, we wish to encourage meaningful green roofs—green roofs that have a story to them—as well as individualistic green roofs—green roofs with personality. If there is one message to come out of this book, it is that making a green roof does not have to be a mysterious or complicated matter, nor does it need to be expensive. Most structures or surfaces open themselves to some sort of greening.

This is the first book that deals specifically with small-scale and domestic green roofs, and we hope it is both inspiring and practical. People who might find this book valuable include:

- home gardeners
- architects
- garden designers
- landscape architects
- self-build or do it yourself (DIY) enthusiasts
- schools, teachers, and parents
- ecologists and nature conservationists

This book is complementary to but very different from other green roof books. Like many landscape, DIY, or garden books, green roof books tend to be authoritative—information is given by experts to the uninitiated. They speak with a single clear confident voice. This book is different. We give some very general and introductory material on construction, planting, and biodiversity, but the main bulk of the book is made up of the real experiences of people and their small-scale green roof projects. It is a human book about the wishes and desires of a wide range of people who have tried to see an idea through to reality. Along the way things have gone wrong, turned out differently, or simply exceeded all expectations.

The book profiles more than forty small- and domestic-scale projects of all shapes and sizes. The projects range from totally self-build to commercially built systems and an array of possibilities in between. They include green roofs on sheds, garden offices, studios, garages, houses, bicycle sheds, and other small structures, as well as several community projects. For each project, details are given for design, construction, and installation, as well as how to plant and look after a green roof. But we have also tried to include a flavour of what motivates people to have a green roof in the first place, whether it has lived up to their expectations, and, in the light of having done it, what lessons they have learned. Don't just take our word for how wonderful and straight-forward having your own green roof is, listen to the people who have had a go for themselves.

We four authors have all come to be passionate about green roofs to a greater or lesser extent because of our experience with the small-scale, intimate, and low-tech methods and approaches described in this book. We all come to the subject from various backgrounds and from different angles, but we are all united in our belief that there is huge untapped potential in creating green roofs at the domestic scale. Indeed, we all came into the green roof world somewhat by accident and as a result of other interests, and then became hooked.

Nigel Dunnett is a university researcher and director of The Green Roof Centre, Sheffield, United Kingdom. He has a botanical and ecologi-

The design possibilities of small-scale green roofs are endless. Here different growing materials and planting mixes produce striking patterns. Photo by Jeff Sorrill

cal background and, as part of his work, he undertakes rigorous scientific trials and evaluations of plants for green roofs. But he is a keen horticulturist and home gardener, and he first became interested in green roofs when faced with an ugly shed in the garden of a new house that he moved into in 1999. Nigel began to think about the numerous exciting green roof planting opportunities there were in the average backyard and started to try out as many different plants as he could. Now, as well as doing research, he consults on and designs green roof plantings, large and small.

Dusty Gedge has been the pioneer in popularizing green roofs in the United Kingdom and runs the main U.K. green roofs website, Livingroofs.org. But he initially came to green roofs, in the late 1990s, through his great interest in bird watching and urban nature. Dusty saw green roofs as a way of compensating for the loss of habitats on the ground when development takes place. Since then, working very closely with researchers in Switzerland, he has brought the concept of designing and making green roofs for their wildlife benefit into the mainstream and is a tireless advocate for green roofs.

John Little is a landscape contractor and designer whose work has a strong community focus. He became interested in green roofs when researching his own self-build house (which won the Daily Telegraph Self-Build House of the Year Award in 1996), as his architect had previously made several turf-roofed buildings. After that there was no turning back. Since then John founded the Grass Roof Company, which specializes in making distinctive small buildings with green roofs of many different types.

Ed Snodgrass, who has a previous background working in youth educational programmes in very challenging social areas in Baltimore, also had a farm in Maryland, which grew maize but was not making much of a return. He had heard about green roofs when they were first being introduced to the United States, and it occurred to him that he might make more out of his land by growing green roof plants rather than traditional crops. Now Ed's green roof nursery, Emory Knoll Farms, is the largest supplier of green roof plants in North America. Ed is continually on the lookout for new reliable green roof plants.

Green Roofs at the Small Scale

Green roofs are simply roofs that have had a layer of vegetation added to them. They are best known when used on the large scale: offices, factories, and other big buildings. The opportunities at a small and residential scale are equally great but have tended to be overshadowed by their larger counterparts. House roofs, garden sheds, porches, summerhouses, balconies, garages, and small extensions offer great potential for planting green roofs. A walk down any typical street will immediately reveal a whole host of opportunities. Creative use of green roofs can transform run-of-the-mill structures into the central focus of a garden. Sheds can be extremely ugly, especially when viewed from above. Indeed, most people who live in towns and cities look out onto expanses of black or grey bitumen and asphalt roofs in their own gardens or those of their neighbours. Greening

At the residential and domestic scale, opportunities for green roofs abound, both on a house and on the structures and buildings around it. Photo by Nigel Dunnett

up these surfaces not only improves the view, but it also makes functional, utilitarian buildings into attractive focal points and features in their own right. Indeed, where garden or outdoor space is very small or restricted, a green roof might be the only chance for bringing plants and wildlife into otherwise hard or built surroundings.

Outside of the house and garden there are many additional opportunities for small-scale green roof structures. These include buildings in schools and educational institutions, community facilities, small-scale pavilions, overhead canopies, and transport shelters. Although interest in green roofs at this scale is great—for example, the major horticulture and garden shows regularly feature buildings with green roofs—as yet there is little guidance available to people about how to do it. And there is certainly very little material available to provide design inspiration for small-scale green roofs.

Green Roof or Roof Garden?

When is a green roof not a green roof but a roof garden? What is the difference, and does it matter? There are countless books devoted to roof

A roof terrace which supports green roof planting, rather than plants in containers or raised beds. Photo by Nigel Dunnett

Different terminology may be used in different regions to describe a green roof. The term *living roof* is used widely, particularly when a roof is designed for wildlife and habitat objectives. An unirrigated green roof may not be green all the time. Using the term *living roof* overcomes false expectations of continuous green, but also implies that the roof is a complete system, supporting more than just plants and including the birds and invertebrates that visit it and the microorganisms in the soil below it. For the same reason, *ecoroof* is also a frequently used term.

gardens and roof terraces. It is very easy to get bogged down in terminology and to emphasize minute differences in different types of green roof, so we will try to avoid rigid categorizations and classifications.

Roof gardens have plants growing in containers or in raised beds. Their role is largely recreational and aesthetic. Typically, a high proportion of the space is unvegetated but is instead paved or decked. The garden tends to require a high degree of maintenance, and the plants require watering and fertilizing.

A green roof, which may also be accessible and have a recreational and aesthetic function, tends to be predominantly vegetated rather than paved. In most cases, the vegetated or soil-covered areas cover the whole roof. Rather than being grown in individual containers, the plants are in a more continuous layer of soil or growing medium, which allows interaction between the plants and is more akin to a natural system.

Types of green roof

Green roofs can vary radically in appearance, largely depending on the depth of the growing medium and the amount of resources (including fertilization and irrigation) that are available for their upkeep. Green roofs with a greater depth of growing medium, say, 250 mm (10 in) and above, can support trees, shrubs, lawns, and water features: all the components of a garden on the ground. Such roofs are really akin to roof gardens and are mostly designed for aesthetic and recreational use. They require a great deal of underlying structural support and a good amount of resources and maintenance to keep them in good condition. These roofs are intensive in their use of resources and largely fall outside the scope of this book.

Green roofs with relatively thin layers (50–200 mm, 2–8 in) of growing medium are much more lightweight and will generally only support lower-growing herbaceous vegetation, small bulbs, and annuals. Maintenance is relatively low—a little resource can be spread over a large area—and these are generally referred to as extensive green roofs. Such roofs are usually installed to achieve a range of environmental objectives and are considered to be much more sustainable.

Some of the most interesting green roof designs break down the distinctions between these two green roof types. For example, when an extensive green roof approach and aesthetic is applied to a recreational roof garden to create an outdoor space rich in visual interest, high biodiversity value, but low in resource inputs, the results can be intriguing and spectacular. Examples of such projects include Wendy Allen's small London roof terrace and Lisa Goode's Manhattan apartment.

Defining Small-Scale and DIY Green Roofs

In this book, we are considering roofs that have a genuine sense of ownership and involvement by the people that use the roofs on an everyday basis: situations in which there is a real connection between people and the green roof. There is a good degree of input into the roof by the owners, even though they may not have made it themselves. And we are looking at examples in which the scale is intimate and human, rather than gigantic and corporate. These projects include a green roof on a new house or an extension to an existing house; recreational roof terraces employing green roof principles; garages or other large outbuildings; garden sheds, offices, and studios and other structures in a garden that can support a green roof; and small-scale buildings and structures in community sites and schools.

Getting Back to Basics

When we make small-scale or DIY green roofs, we are going right back to the roots of the green roof idea. The original Scandinavian pitched turf or sod roofs were, and are, highly sustainable. They used local materials (often directly from the site) and simple technology to make an effective and inexpensive insulation and protective layer. In so doing, they also replaced vegetation and green that was removed at ground level. But equally importantly, they were small in scale—covering the individual dwelling or maybe the community meeting house—and they could be made and repaired by the local craftsman or even the people who lived in the building. The structure was built to take the load, and enough soil was put up on the roof to make sure the plants survived. Because

This accessible green roof near Asheville, North Carolina, United States, is located off the main floor of the house, on top of the lower guest wing. The green roof has150 mm (6 in) of growing medium and is planted with a variety of native and ornamental perennials and grasses to unify it with the surrounding pastoral and meadow landscape and mountain views. A subsurface irrigation system is tied into the rainwater harvesting system of the house. Photos by Emilio Ancaya, Living Roofs, Inc.

Left: Green-roofed garages for an apartment block in Sheffield, United Kingdom. Photo by Nigel Dunnett

Below left: A green roof on a carport and wood store. Photo by John Little

Below: The scope for greening small surfaces is endless. Photo by Nigel Dunnett

Above left: A greened roof on a bus shelter in Sheffield, United Kingdom, created with a pregrown sedum mat. Photo by Groundwork Sheffield

Above: A fragment of sedum mat fitted over a bird house. Photo by Nigel Dunnett

Left: A traditional building on Orkney, Scotland, with the same grass community as on the ground growing in a peaty soil on the roof. Photo by Richard Hoare

the buildings were built to function and materials were inexpensive or free and local, current concerns about cost and loadings did not really arise.

Modern green roof systems were developed in very different circumstances. Arising in continental Europe in major commercial and industrial centres, they were applied widely on municipal, public, and commercial buildings which were built using modern construction techniques. Crucially, the roofs were invariably flat. Because the roofs of many modern buildings are not built to take huge loadings, the green roof systems had to be lightweight. Getting water off the flat roof was essential. Water captured in the growing medium added additional loading, and ponding or puddling on the roof surface was potentially detrimental to the roof itself, because the highly drought-tolerant plants adapted to thin and lightweight green roof systems were not happy sitting in waterlogged soil, particularly over winter. Because of the high cost of modern buildings, green roofs had to be reliable and fail-safe. The most commonly used modern commercial green roof systems have therefore developed as standardized

Modern Norwegian cabins in the traditional style, with grass roofs. Photo by Nigel Dunnett

products made on an industrial scale, with a high degree of dependability and reliability, if installed correctly. Modern green roofs are triumphs of efficient technology and are often very technological in themselves, consisting of layers of manufactured components. This may also include the vegetation, which is often mass produced as pregrown mats. These green roofs have to work correctly, and they have to work on a large scale.

As these commercial systems were developed, however, there has also been a continuing interest in small-scale and low-tech approaches, taking us right back to the start of the idea. Grass roofs have long been part of green or eco-building traditions and have tended to be much more akin to the traditional Scandinavian model than the modern lightweight systems. Whereas earlier examples were often restricted to eco-settlements or demonstration buildings, in the past decade there has been a renewed interest from landscape and garden designers in the creative and aesthetic potential of green-roofed garden buildings and structures, which is bringing green roofs into the horticultural mainstream. In addition, a change in working practices has seen more people working from home and a rise in the numbers of garden offices and studios, many of which have

The green roof on the Minneapolis Library includes a high proportion of species native to the region. The plants are growing in artificial lightweight soil, with drainage and protection layers beneath. Photo by Nigel Dunnett

a strong design sensibility, as opposed to the standard summerhouses of former times. Green roofs are easily incorporated into such structures. But perhaps one of the greatest boosts to the popularity of small-scale green roofs has been the development of ideas relating to green roofs and biodiversity. As discussed later in the book, this approach, arising from the ideas of Stephan Brenneisen in Switzerland and applied in London by Dusty Gedge, has challenged the concept of uniform lightweight standardized green roofs that have no sense of place. Instead, each roof is seen as unique, and the depth of the growing medium varies. This alternative viewpoint has been taken up enthusiastically by many small-scale and domestic green roof owners.

Green Roof Benefits

One reason for the increasing popularity of green roofs is that they deliver a wide range of environmental and human benefits. The general benefits of green roofs are becoming widely known, and we will not go into great detail here. For a full discussion of benefits and up-to-date descriptions of the research evidence that backs them up, we refer you to *Planting Green Roofs and Living Walls* by Nigel Dunnett and Noël Kingsbury (Timber Press, 2008) and *The Green Roof Manual* by Ed Snodgrass and Linda McIntyre (Timber Press, 2010).

The aesthetic benefits of adding exciting plantings to rooftops and bringing previously sterile surfaces back to life are clear. Other important green roof benefits include:

- rainwater management
- cooling and energy conservation
- increasing biodiversity
- providing wildlife habitat
- noise insulation
- waste water treatment
- food production

Claims are made about the potential benefit of green roofs in trapping atmospheric air pollution and their value as sinks for atmospheric carbon

A self-built garden studio. Photo by David Whyte, Greentide

Right and below: Earth-sheltered buildings, such as the Nine Houses project in Switzerland, extend the concept of plants on buildings. Photos by Ben Nicholson

Below right: A beautiful garden room in Kennett Square, Pennsylvania, United States. Photo by Ed Snodgrass

dioxide. While these claims may be valid, the benefits only arise as a result of large-scale greening, and small green roofs are likely to have a minimal effect.

Rainwater management

Green roofs act like giant sponges, soaking up and slowly releasing the rain that falls on them. Most research indicates that at least half of all the water that falls on a green roof over the course of a year never makes it down to ground level. As such, green roofs are a valuable tool in reducing the amount of water running off hard impervious surfaces following a heavy rain, thereby reducing pressure on urban drainage systems and lessening the risk of flooding and overload of those systems. Green roofs are only part of a series of other landscape-based water management features, including bioswales, rain gardens, and detention ponds, and definitely do not provide the complete solution.

At a city level, green roofs will only make a real impact if a large proportion of rooftops are greened. At the local and neighbourhood scales, however, a green roof can make a definite difference to the amount of water running off a site. The sheer number of dwellings and gardens in urban areas means that if a good proportion of small-scale structures can be greened, then the total effect may become significant.

At the individual garden level, a green roof is a fine starting point for a zero-runoff garden, in which every drop of rainwater that falls onto it is retained within it. Artful rainwater design can be the basis of a complete garden, with other features such as stormwater planters, rain gardens, and bioswales forming the main components. A full discussion of rain gardens and creative rainwater management can be found in *Rain Gardens: Managing Water Sustainability in the Garden and Designed Landscape* by Nigel Dunnett and Andy Clayden (Timber Press, 2007).

Cooling and energy conservation

A tangible benefit for small-scale structures is the potential cooling effect of a green roof. The combination of shading the roof by the substrate and vegetation and the cooling effect of water evaporating off the plants means that a green-roofed building effectively sweats and cools the air

Green roof benefits

Growing vegetables, herbs, and fruit

Promoting biodiversity
   Creating new habitats
   Supporting native plants
    and animals

Horticulture and growing plants

Water
   Reducing rainwater runoff
   Cleaning rainwater

Protecting waterproofing

Sound insulation

Aesthetic
   Beauty
   Well-being

Energy
   Summer cooling
   Winter insulation

Reducing heat reflection

Capturing carbon

around it. This makes it much more comfortable to be in the building and potentially will cut down on the power consumption for air conditioning. Much more research needs to be done in this area, but preliminary work suggests at least a 10 percent reduction in energy bills for cooling a room beneath a green roof. (There is much less evidence of a green roof keeping a building warmer in the winter. The wet substrate tends to have little insulating value, unless a good depth of substrate is used.)

Green roofs are frequently also included in discussions relating to reducing the urban heat island through covering up bare hard surfaces that absorb and reflect the sun's warmth back into the atmosphere. For this to be effective, large-scale roof greening would need to be employed on large buildings. Greening individual small-scale structures will have little overall impact, unless we can green as many of them as possible.

Biodiversity and wildlife habitat

Increasing biodiversity and providing habitat for wildlife are clear and obvious benefits that even the smallest green roof can sign up to.

This small green roof on a factory building in China produces 'cut and come again' greens. Photo by Ruijue Hue

Replacing a dead surface with a living one is an automatic increase in value. Increasing biodiversity simply means increasing the variety of living things in any area. Putting plants onto a rooftop will also lead to an increase in animal life. Flowering plants will encourage insects such as bees and butterflies to feed on the nectar. Seed-eating birds such as finches and sparrows will come in autumn and over the winter. Beetles, spiders, and other invertebrates will make their homes among the foliage. But it's not just animals that are drawn in: green roofs can be havens for rare plants or for native plants that are typical of your region.

Noise insulation

As we interviewed the owners of small-scale green roof projects, many people responded that the green roof muffles out noise. Again, there has been little in-depth research into this aspect.

Waste water treatment

It may be possible to use roof-level planting to clean and filter grey water from a house by pumping and circulating the water through a rooftop wetland. Certainly in arid regions it may not be possible to irrigate a green roof with potable water. Circulating water over a rooftop will cause it to act like a living heat exchanger, maximizing the cooling benefit. While some large-scale examples exist of rooftop water treatment wetlands, this has yet to be applied at the smaller scale.

Food production

Growing food on rooftops has huge potential, and one that is only just being realized. It may soon become a necessity as pressure for local urban food production increases. Green roof design and planting has largely been unproductive until now, but there is great interest in utilizing all the unused space on urban rooftops for locally produced fruit and vegetables. Herbs, salad greens, and larger crops may all be grown successfully. The green roofs described in the projects section include several inspiring examples.

MAKING A GREEN ROOF

GREEN ROOFS are a simple concept. If you can keep the plants and soil on the roof and let the excess water off, you have a green roof. If that's all you knew about green roofs before you built one, you would still have a roof that will deliver nearly all the benefits in terms of ecology, cooling, and sustainable drainage without, perhaps, the subtleties and aesthetics of a well-planned roof. Green roofs always offer more than any other roof covering, no matter how basic they may be.

This book is about getting back to basics. Making a green roof nowadays can seem hugely complicated and expensive, with a bewildering array of different products and systems available and an insurmountable choice of options for materials, installation, and planting. And even when the roof is up, there is the worry of keeping it there and having to look after it forever. It is little wonder that green roofs are still not very common.

Plants can often be seen growing naturally, but sparsely, on old roof surfaces and wall tops, with apparently very little to support them. In fact, the modern green roof technologies originated in Germany after people noticed that sedums and grasses naturally colonized layers of sand and ballast that were spread over flat roofs to protect the waterproof layer from damage and that the plant layer seemed to give additional benefits. It does not require too much more effort to actively create suitable conditions on a roof for plants to thrive.

DIY or Green Roof Company?

Having decided to have a green roof, you are faced with the choice of how to do it. Should you employ a green roof company to do the whole job, or do it yourself? Or should you get someone else to do most of it, but put in all the plants yourself? Particularly for people who do not see themselves as amateur builders or DIY experts, the decision to make a green roof can be a daunting one.

The roof structure on this yoga studio in Cornwall, United Kingdom, consists of oak logs. Local soil and turf was used to make the grass roof. Photos by Katy Bryce

Commercial green roof companies and system providers

Fortunately the choice is actually not that difficult. For some projects the decision will be clear. To put a green roof on a house or significant extension, specialist advice must be sought, and a roofing contractor will be used anyway. The waterproofing must work, and building regulations must be met. The roof surface may be inaccessible or generally unsafe to work on. For significant newly built or retrofitted projects, it is definitely worthwhile for you or the architect to obtain specialist advice from a commercial green roof supplier. If a green roof uses a commercial system, then the green roof company will usually provide a long-term warranty against any problems, provided an approved contractor was used to install the roof.

However, the major green roof companies will not be interested in anything other than relatively large projects, one on a new house, for example. Anything smaller will just not be cost-effective. Garden sheds and garages will be too small for them to even consider. It may still be possible to find a contractor who will install a green roof for you, but we advise that you choose very carefully. Increasingly we hear stories of general roofing contractors offering a green roofing service. But all too often

Below: *Sedum album* growing naturally in the hollows of an old corrugated metal roof, Sheffield, United Kingdom. Photo by Nigel Dunnett

Below right: *Sedum reflexum* is thriving in the shade on this old stone roof in Derbyshire, United Kingdom, while mosses dominate in the sun. Photo by Nigel Dunnett

this can be opportunistic and based on little understanding of the system. Insist on seeing testimonials and examples of previous work and, where possible, evidence of training in the field. In North America, a certified training programme for green roof professionals is offered by the organization Green Roofs for Healthy Cities, and contractors who have attended and been awarded the certificate will have a good basic knowledge of the field.

Dedicated green roof contractors

For absolute confidence, choose a dedicated company with demonstrated expertise, experience, and a good track record. Two such companies in the United Kingdom are the Grass Roof Company, based in the south of England, and Green Estate Ltd., based in Sheffield in the north of England. (John Little is partner in the Grass Roof Company, and Green Estate Ltd. works closely with Nigel Dunnett at Sheffield University.) In the United States, an example is Living Roofs, Inc., based in North Carolina. In addition to offering full design and building, the company will also supply full construction drawings for DIY use, together with a complete listing of the required materials, all of which are all readily available from DIY outlets. Projects from these three companies are featured heavily in this book.

Working with such companies often brings additional rewards. They will be happy to design the roof or to help you design the roof, but they can also have ongoing involvement with the project. For example, the Grass Roof Company does a lot of school and community-based schemes and are very willing to become involved in educational and public events, as well as remaining closely involved with projects for advice and maintenance. Green Estate Ltd. provide a photographic report on maintenance for inaccessible or difficult-to-view roofs.

Both contractor and DIY

The absolutely crucial aspects of constructing a green roof are that the building and roof do not fall down (that is, the underlying structure can support the roof) and the waterproofing is absolutely leak-proof before the green roof goes on top. In many cases and on larger projects, it will

The Shelter, a self-build DIY green roof garden studio from Living Roofs, Inc. All materials are readily available, and complete plans and assembly instructions are provided.

be practical to employ builders, joiners, and roofing contractors if you do not have those skills, and then you can handle the substrate or growing medium and planting. This can work on large-scale and community projects as well as at the smaller scale. For example, a roofing contractor may install the waterproofing, insulation, and drainage components, if required. All work above this can be carried out by you and volunteers, provided all the relevant health, safety, and other procedures, risk assessments, and insurances have been cleared. For example, the green roof on the Sharrow School, Sheffield, was completed with more than 100 volunteers, who spread and mounded substrate and undertook planting and seeding.

Totally DIY

Many of the projects in the book were built without the help of a contractor, and for very small projects there will be no other choice. Dan Cornwell of Green Estate Ltd. notes that it is not cost-effective for them

Building this green roof at the University of Tennessee was a hands-on educational experience for a local high school carpentry class. The class builds a shed every year and sells it to the public to make money for the following year's project. Photo by Emilio Ancaya, Living Roofs, Inc.

to work on installing very small domestic projects, although the company are happy to supply all the materials (such as bags of substrate) and to give advice. In Germany it is common to be able to go to the local garden centre and purchase ready-made green roof kits. In the future, as demand increases for small-scale projects, this will likely be more common in many other countries. But, again, these tend to be standardized products that offer uniform outcome.

To achieve something with a truly individual character and outcome, DIY is the only solution. For small projects, such as a green roof on a bicycle shelter, a garden shed, or other examples in which people are not going to be living beneath the roof, the need to be highly precise about loadings and finishing is less important than on projects for which building regulations must be met. However, care must be taken so that a roof does not collapse.

The outstanding conclusion from the projects in this book is that it is worth having a go. Most people worked with a degree of trial-and-error and experimentation. Everyone has been overwhelmingly pleased with the results, and they often achieved that success following initial doubts or confusion about how to go about it. It is also clear that there is no definitive right way to build a small green roof.

The Building Structure Beneath the Green Roof

In this section we describe some of the basic considerations when designing and installing a green roof, and we look first at the building structure beneath the green roof. The details here are deliberately brief and simply introduce the main components. There is a wealth of detailed material in the projects section that shows exactly how each was constructed.

Weight loading, weight loading, weight loading

Quite simply, it is weight loading that ultimately dictates the quality, functioning, and appearance of a green roof. The more the roof can support, the more design and plant choices you will have. If you are lucky enough to be designing a new structure, then you can build in the weight loading needed for exactly the type of roof that you want. If, however, you are retrofitting an existing roof, then the roof must be checked to see what it can support. This will then determine the plant and substrate choices. The two tables list the weights of a range of materials commonly used on green roofs and the loadings of some of the projects in the book.

These weights are for the maximum saturated loading for a commercial green roof substrate. You will obviously need to check the weight of

The saturated weight of a range of green roof materials

Materials	Weight of a 1-cm layer (kg per square metre)	Weight of a 1-in layer (lb per square foot)
Gravel	16–19	8.4–9.9
Pebbles	19	9.9
Pumice	6.5	3.3
Brick (solid with mortar)	18	9.4
Sand	18–22	9.4–11.4
Sand and gravel mixed	18	9.4
Topsoil	17–20	8.9–10.4
Lava	8	4.1
Perlite	5	2.54
Vermiculite	1	0.51
Light expanded clay aggregate (LECA)	3–4	1.5–2.0
Water	10	5.3

Source: *Planting Green Roofs and Living Walls* by Nigel Dunnett and Noël Kingsbury (Timber Press, 2008)

The weight loading of a few of the green roof projects

Project	Weight	Depth of substrate
Klecha house extension	80 kg/m^2 (16.4 lb/sq ft)	50–75 mm (2–3 in)
Bid and Skil's garden room	130 kg/m^2 (26.7 lb/sq ft)	75–100 mm (3–4 in)
Tricia and DP's shed	200 kg/m^2 (41 lb/sq ft)	100–150 mm (4–6 in)
Herringham outdoor classroom	250 kg/m^2 (51.3 lb/sq ft)	150–175 mm (6–7 in)

the material you choose. If you are dealing with an architect or structural engineer, make sure they realize this is just the weight of the substrate and plants, that is, the green element of the roof build-up. If making a newly built structure, we strongly recommend aiming for a minimum substrate depth of 100 mm (4 in), if you can, and calculating the loading accordingly.

It is important not to be put off by these figures, but also to take them seriously. Weight loading is the only part of a green roof you cannot be flexible with. You can have fun with all the other elements of a green roof, but you must make sure the roof does not collapse.

Walls and support

A green roof adds weight to a building, in effect making it top-heavy. If the walls are timber, then you will need to brace them well to prevent racking (when the walls move out of square) and ensure the walls are rigid. Racking is simple to prevent by either fixing a cross or diagonal brace from corner to corner of a wall or, better still, lining it with sheet

A green-roofed container building in the Rain Garden at The London Wetland Centre. Designed and built by Green Roof Shelters. Photo by Nigel Dunnett

Top left: An existing typical lightweight garden shed can be strengthened to enable it to take a green roof. Each wall panel is braced with horizontal and diagonal batons. Photo by Green Estate Ltd.

Top right: Uprights give additional support. Photo by Green Estate Ltd.

Above: Finally, additional braces strengthen the roof. Photo by Green Estate Ltd.

The completed shed, with green roof tray added on top. Photo by Green Estate Ltd.

material makes the walls rigid. It also means the downward force the structure's timber uprights can handle is greatly increased. Obviously, you will also need to make sure any door, window, or opening in a wall is spanned with a beam sufficient to carry the roof load.

Again, when designing a new structure, it is possible to construct sturdy rigid walls. But modifying an existing structure with more flimsy walls may present a greater challenge. With simple judicious bracing, however, it is possible to convert a typical relatively flimsy shed from a garden centre or DIY store into a structure capable of supporting a 100-mm (4-in) depth of substrate.

An alternative approach to supporting a green roof on an existing building is to support the green roof partially or wholly with external supporting structures. Nigel Dunnett's two sheds employ this technique.

Roof supports (joists, rafters)

The dimensions of the roof supports or joists you use depend on two things: how much weight you intend to put on the roof, and the width of the span the joists need to cross. The heavier the loading, the closer together the joists need to be. The wider the span, the more substantial the roof joists need to be. So, for instance, a roof with a load of 100 kg/m² (20.5 lb/sq ft) spanning, say 2.6 m (8.5 ft), would need 150 × 50 mm (6 × 2 in) timbers spaced at 400 mm (16 in) apart.

Roof deck

The roof deck is the continuous flat surface that supports the additional layers of the green roof on top of it. On flat-roofed houses or more substantial structures, the roof deck may be concrete (which can usually support significant loading), metal (which is often not able to support significant loading without additional strengthening), wood, or other materials. On self-built, DIY, and smaller projects the roof deck is likely to be wood. Typically this will be a minimum of 20-mm (0.75-in) sheet material such as plywood or strand board or 20- to 25-mm (0.75- to 1.0-in) planking. You now have a platform strong enough to support the roof.

For houses, extensions, or garden buildings and offices that people will be using regularly, it will also be necessary to consider insulation. Most commonly, a warm roof build-up will be used, whereby an insulation layer is placed on top of the roof deck and then the waterproofing layer is placed on top of that. You may also need to consider a vapour control layer that lets water vapour out of the roof, rather than it condensing within the roof and causing dampness. For most other applications in which people are not regularly using the building, these additional layers are not necessary. The waterproofing can be installed directly on the roof deck.

Waterproofing

Proper waterproofing is absolutely essential to a successful green roof. A leaking roof beneath a green roof can be a major problem—both in finding the leak and in having to take up the green roof to mend it. After you have put plants and soil on the roof, the last thing you want is for the roof to leak.

It is important to note that roofing felt and asphalt, some of the most common roofing materials used on small-scale structures, are not suitable as a waterproofing base. The joins between the felt sheets are very easily exploited by plant roots, and the material will weaken under a layer of soil and plants. Such materials must be covered by another layer, such as a flexible liner.

The two most common waterproofing techniques are using a flexible liner or a liquid painted or spray-on waterproofing material. For most small-scale projects, a liner is the easiest solution. Such a roof is often referred to as a single-ply roof. The most durable material is a synthetic rubber liner. Professional roofers use EPDM, a material that is long-lasting and very weather resistant, and doesn't become brittle on exposure to light, unlike many other lining materials. For most large green roof projects it should be possible to get a sheet prefabricated offsite that covers the entire roof. EPDM is not widely available to the nonprofessional, however, and is usually installed by qualified contractors. Luckily, for smaller projects, butyl rubber is widely available from DIY stores and garden centres as pond lining. We advise you to try and buy the best quality you can afford. Butyl rubber will deteriorate if exposed to sunlight over long

Page 39: Installing a green roof on a terrace row of new-build bungalows in Sheffield, United Kingdom. Photos by Green Estate Ltd.

Top left: A plywood roof with insulation panels is ready to be laid.

Top right: The insulation in place

Center left: The waterproofing is sealed on top of the insulation.

Center right: The drainage mat is laid over a protective geotextile.

Bottom left: A filter sheet sits on top of the drainage mat, and substrate is spread on top of this.

Bottom right: The completed bungalow green roofs. A pebble strip divides each roof from the adjacent, giving a sense of separate dwellings beneath.

GREEN ROOFS PROTECT THE WATERPROOFING

Putting plants and soil on top of the waterproofing layer is actually good, because it protects the material from ultraviolet radiation and the stresses caused by excessive hot and cold temperatures, which will make the material last longer. In fact, the origins of green roofs come from this protecting property. The original Scandinavian turf roofs were green to protect the birch-bark waterproofing. The Germans who started the modern green roof movement used sand to protect the early bitumen roofs from fire. This sand vegetated naturally, and the first German green roofs were born.

periods—it is therefore important that the liner is completely covered with substrate or other material. Whatever material you use, make sure it has root protection, that is, it is designed to resist the ingress of roots as the plants grow. There are many commercial liners available that carry a warranty of twenty to twenty-five years.

You may object to the use of such liners on environmental grounds, for example, because of the energy and the waste products involved in their manufacture. Alternatives may be available, and such alternative materials were used on the Wheeler Street Leangreen House project. Whatever waterproofing material you use, it will need protecting top and bottom with a puncture-resistant felt (geotextile) or other material in the same way you would protect a pond liner from damage. While this protection is important in the long-term, it is critical when working on the roof during the construction phase, and great care must be taken when walking on the exposed waterproofing layer.

Edges and edgings

Once the waterproofing is in place, the final stage is to ensure that the growing medium and plants remain in place on the roof. On a small-scale project, the edge detail can really make the roof. The edging is the bit that is seen from below or from the side, and it is therefore worth making the edging look good. Whatever method you choose, you must separate the substrate from the roof edge with some sort of filter sheet or geotextile. This allows water through without all the fines from the substrate being washed out from the roof. The projects show many examples of edging details.

The Green Roof Build-Up

In considering green roofs, we look at both what goes into a typical commercial system and how DIY versions may differ from that. Most professionals consider that a green roof starts from the waterproofing layer upwards. This is essentially what differs between a green roof and a conventional roof, and it is also what is required to support the growth of plants.

Above: Waterproofing a round conical roof with a flexible liner on a building at a school in Sheffield, United Kingdom. Photo by Green Estate Ltd.

Right: The finished building. Photo by Green Estate Ltd.

Right: An old Swedish farmhouse with a grass roof. Photo by Nigel Dunnett

Above: The edging on the traditional Scandinavian roofs was very simple: a wooden beam pegged in place to prevent soil and plants slipping off the roof. Photo by Nigel Dunnett

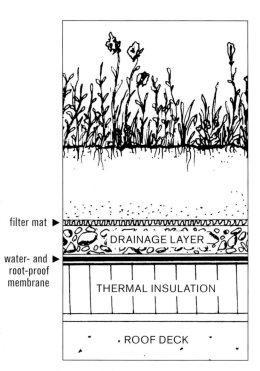

filter mat ▶

water- and ▶
root-proof
membrane

DRAINAGE LAYER

THERMAL INSULATION

· ROOF DECK

Section through a typical green roof.
The thermal insulation layer is only
necessary where insulation is required.
Drawing by Hay Joung Hwang

Proper drainage

Most drought-tolerant plants suitable for a green roof dislike their roots sitting in water during the cold of winter or during the heat of summer in humid zones. It is important that excess water is allowed to drain off the roof in the same way that you would put drainage in the bottom of a container plant.

Commercial drainage mats are available. These are usually plastic layers that look like small, flat, open egg boxes which capture and store rainwater and then release the excess when the cells are full. They lift the green roof off the roof deck surface. On a flat roof, drainage mats are useful to even out any fluctuations in level and to raise the substrate above areas that might be subject to ponding or water collection. The plastic drainage layer can be replaced with a layer of aggregate, such as gravel or stone (both relatively heavy) or expanded clay or shale. Whatever is used, the drainage layer must be separated from the substrate so that the soil does not wash down into the drainage material and cause it to become blocked. A geotextile filter sheet will do the job.

The commercial drainage layer systems were developed to deal with flat roofs, with relatively shallow substrate depths such that water had to be removed from the system. On small-scale and DIY structures, it is questionable whether such a layer is really necessary. If possible, it would be better to increase the depth of the substrate so that more water could be stored within the substrate, if stormwater amelioration is an important consideration.

In the case of a sloped roof, the justification for a separate drainage layer disappears. If the roof slope is above, say, 5°, it is unlikely you will need to worry about this layer because the excess water will drain easily from the slope. Once the water reaches the lower edge of the roof, it can simply drip off, run into a gutter, or, if you have an internal outlet, escape down a rain chain.

Typically on larger roofs, pebbles or stones are used along the edge of the roof, as well as around skylights, chimneys, flues, and anything which protrudes from the surface. This material keeps an area free of vegetation to aid water movement to the drainage outlets.

You may wish to experiment with drainage. Where drainage is

Installing a green roof on a flat-roofed garage. Photos by Green Estate Ltd.

Top left: A flexible rubber liner draped over a garage roof and temporarily held in place with bags of substrate.

Top right: A geotextile protective layer has been laid on top of the liner, and a drainage mat is being laid on top of that. Note how the waterproof liner also covers the section of the house wall adjoining the green roof.

Above left: Another geotextile filter sheet is placed on top of the drainage layer, and then substrate can be spread.

Above: The finished roof, with the top of the liner hidden under coping stones.

Left: A pebble edge leads to the existing roof drainage point. Photo by Green Estate Ltd.

Above: A rain chain directs water from the roof to a point on the ground and makes a striking visual feature in itself. Photo by Ed Snodgrass

Left: An edging of pebbles and log sections on this green roof on a converted shipping container retains substrate, aids drainage, provides invertebrate habitat, and is an attractive feature in itself. Photo by John Little

Page 45: On Nigel Dunnett's shed roof, the substrate is retained with stacked flat stones. The mixed planting contains annuals, sedums, grasses, perennials, and bulbs. Photo by Nigel Dunnett

impeded or prevented, very different vegetation can develop on a roof that may otherwise be restricted to drought-tolerant plants. There is no practical reason, apart from loading restrictions, as to why wetland areas cannot develop on a roof. Andy Clayden's garden room and Ben and Charlotte Foulton's house extension show what happens when drainage conditions change across a roof.

Substrate and growing medium

Although a great amount of work has been done to formulate specific green roof mixes, the original Scandinavian green roofs used natural soil, and many current green roofs also use natural soils and subsoils. Some kind of plant will grow no matter what medium you choose. But there are two important considerations here. First, natural soils are very heavy compared with the artificial green roof substrates or growing media which have been developed specifically to reduce the weight loading of a green roof. Second, a standard soil may not allow you to grow the plants you want. For a particular desired effect, it is important to choose the substrate carefully.

For growing typical drought-tolerant plants such as alpines, sedums, and other succulents or species-rich wildflower meadows, it is important that the growing medium is free-draining. Typical commercial green roof substrates consist mainly of a granular mineral component (80–90 percent). Commonly used components are crushed brick, pumice, expanded clay, or expanded shale. Organic material is also added to store moisture and make nutrients available. Although peat is widely used in other countries, in the United Kingdom it has become virtually unacceptable as a medium because of overexploitation of peat reserves and associated habitat destruction. Green waste compost is being used increasingly, as are coconut coir and composed bark.

Commercial substrates have been developed to deliver a reliable, standard, and uniform product—something that is essential on costly large-scale commercial schemes. But the move towards greater ecological thinking in green roof design has led to the consideration of different substrate materials. Partly this is related to a desire to use locally sourced materials and waste products rather than new materials which require a

SOME DESIGN IDEAS

- To create an interesting diverse roof, try varying the type and depth of your substrate.
- Generally avoid nutrient-rich material—this will encourage weeds and rank growth—unless that is what you want.
- To create a garden roof, try to get a depth of at least 150 mm (6 in) and be prepared to spend time maintaining to keep the garden feel.
- In general, deeper, low-nutrient substrates seem to work best if you want to develop really interesting green roof vegetation.

lot of energy for their manufacture or which must be transported great distances. But using various materials is also partly related to the desire to create different ecological conditions and habitats on a roof. So, to create calcareous grassland green roofs, for example, chalk or limestone may be used as part or all of the mix. On small-scale projects you will have the chance to experiment with materials that come to hand. For example, several of the projects that involved John Little and the Grass Roof Company used waste crushed ceramics (old sinks, basins, and toilets). Sands, gravels, stones, and pebbles can all be used.

Different types of plantings require different substrates. If the roof's loading tolerances will allow, you may wish to grow larger perennials as well as alpines or maybe even some vegetables. Here a substrate higher in organic matter will be essential for greater moisture conservation, and you will also need a substrate depth of up to 200 mm (8 in).

Whatever materials you choose, make sure the depths and subsequent weight loading fits with your structure. And then have fun!

Modular systems

An alternative approach to putting plants and substrate onto a green roof is to use modules. These are preplanted trays that can be lifted into position on the waterproofed roof surface. One advantage of modules is that they are flexible: trays can be lifted, removed, or repositioned. Another is that an instant effect is possible. You can make your own modules relatively easily. Because they are small containers, however, root growth and spread of the plants is more restricted than if growing on an integrated green roof surface. Therefore, the need for fertilizer applications in the long-term may be higher.

Irrigation

Whether or not to incorporate irrigation presents a dilemma to many people. Green roofs are supposed to be all about water management, so why add mains, tap, or potable water to them? On the other hand, if all the plants on a green roof die, then its functioning will be severely reduced, and it could hardly be called a green or living roof any longer.

Most of the projects in this book aim to avoid irrigation or to keep it to an absolute minimum. This makes ecological and horticultural sense: Plants that are regularly irrigated become dependent on irrigation, whereas plants that are irrigated only in extremes are much more stress tolerant. Where water availability is a serious issue, plant choices must maximize drought tolerance. Plants will need to have water available for their establishment, but thereafter it is less necessary.

If irrigation is to be provided, then a submerged pipe or drip line should be used rather than an overhead sprinkler. Also, the irrigation should be on a controlled timer, or it should be possible to turn it on only when needed. On a small and domestic scale, however, water can be applied by hand using a watering can or hose if required in very extreme events. By far the best practice is to use harvested rainwater collected in a cistern or water butt (cistern), or to use grey recycled water from wash basins, baths, or showers.

In regions where water conservation is crucial because of long-term and regular drought, it may be mandatory to collect or harvest water from the roof. A green roof will obviously significantly reduce the amount of water coming off the roof. Although the water may be discoloured it will be perfectly safe for nonpotable uses. It is advisable in these circumstances, however, to green only a proportion of the total roof surface so that there is some surface remaining for rainwater harvesting.

Preplanted modules at Emory Knoll Farms, ready for use on a rooftop. Photo by Nigel Dunnett

PLANTING GREEN ROOFS

And now for the fun part, and in some ways the most important part of a green roof: the plants. The planting on the roof is what, after all, defines a green roof. At the small scale, where roofs are visible and accessible, there is a chance to really experiment with the planting of the roof. In small spaces, a green roof on a garden structure may be the only chance there is for growing plants. A good many reliable tried-and-tested species will put up with the difficult conditions on a green roof. However, for people who have an interest in horticulture, plants, gardens, and ecology, green roofs offer great scope for experimentation. We have still only explored a fraction of the possible plants that could be used on green roofs, and small-scale and garden green roofs offer an excellent opportunity to try out more. Green roofs may also be productive. As more and more people in towns and cities turn to growing their own food, the rooftop offers a chance to grow many of our most familiar herbs and perhaps more substantial crops as well.

Roofs covered purely in substrate or aggregate will still provide some of the benefits that green roofs are known for, but the plant layer will enhance and magnify those benefits. Plants protect the substrate layer from leaching and erosion; they trap, absorb, and evaporate rainwater; they contribute to cooling of the roof surface; they provide food and habitat for invertebrates and birds; and they aid in the capture of air pollutants and provide a sink for atmospheric carbon. At the small scale, where roofs are visible and accessible, plants provide aesthetic appeal. The type and extent of vegetation determines the visual character and quality of the roof. Successful vegetation establishment is therefore central to a successful green roof.

The green roof environment is a particularly harsh one for plant growth, providing very shallow growing medium, limited water and nutrient availability, and increased exposure to wind and intense sunlight. But it is not an impossible environment, and a large number of plants are well adapted to coping with drought stress or very shallow soils, because

Purple chives (*Allium schoenoprasum*) in full flower on a green roof. Photo by Nigel Dunnett

Below: *Sedum album* growing naturally in stony shingle on Dungeness in Kent, United Kingdom. The area gets very little rainfall, and the plants grow in free-draining stones. The conditions and appearance are much like a green roof, and the vegetation is similar to that commonly used on green roofs. Photo by Nigel Dunnett

Below right: Harebells (*Campanula rotundifolia*) and fescue grasses growing in thin soil pockets on bare rock on a coastal cliff. Photo by Nigel Dunnett

the places that they grow naturally are very similar: rocky cliffs, sandy or shingly areas, and dry grasslands, for example.

Plants suitable for green roofs must be easy to establish, stay on the roof over time (either through being tough, hardy, and relatively long-lived or by regenerating easily from seed or vegetatively), and have low maintenance requirements. Many green roof plants have a relatively low and spreading growth form and are therefore effective at covering the surface. Beyond these considerations, more specific plant choices may be related to a particular function or type of roof: the aesthetic qualities of the plant, whether it provides a food source for invertebrates, or whether it is characteristic of a particular habitat or region, for example.

Sedums are, with good reason, the most widely used plants for green roofs. They are supremely drought-resistant and able to grow in shallow, free-draining substrates. Indeed, many sedums grow naturally on bare rock surfaces and on sands and gravels. Sedums were widely used in the early days of the development of extensive green roofs precisely because

they naturally colonized aggregate-covered flat roofs. However, the range of potential plants goes far beyond sedums.

For much more detailed discussions of plants for green roofs, we recommend *Green Roof Plants* by Ed and Lucie Snodgrass (Timber Press, 2006) and *Planting Green Roofs and Living Walls* by Nigel Dunnett and Noël Kingsbury (Timber Press, 2008).

Green Roof Plant Types

The depth of the growing medium is the single greatest deciding factor on what can be grown on a green roof. On very shallow depths of substrate (less than 50 mm, 2 in), only the toughest and most specialized species will survive, and the growth of those will be sparse and stressed where growing medium is especially thin. We always aim to achieve a minimum growing medium depth of at least 100 mm (4 in) where this is possible. If substrate depth can be increased, then the range of potential plants also increases. But greater substrate depth brings with it two problems: the loading on the roof increases, and conditions start to become very favourable for a wide range of plants, including weeds, and you have a greater need for maintenance to keep your desired plantings in place. For this reason, we recommend using a substrate that is not high in nutrients even at the greater depths, unless required for a specific purpose, such as growing vegetables. Once substrate depths increase beyond 250 mm (10 in), we are moving into the territory of the conventional roof garden, involving trees, shrubs, bushes, lush lawns, and so on, and this is really outside the scope of this book.

Succulents and sedums

Succulent species store water in their leaves and have considerable moisture-conserving abilities. The succulents most commonly used on green roofs are sedums: mostly evergreens, with year-round plant cover and a wide variety of leaf shapes and colours. Most *Sedum* species flower in May and June, and the common flower colours are yellow or pale pink. Reliable and widely used species include *Sedum album, Sedum acre*, and *Sedum rupestre*. These species all have relatively small leaves, as does

Sedum spurium in flower.
Photo by Nigel Dunnett

Above: Sedums planted in wide bands in summer at Emory Knoll Farms. Photo by Ed Snodgrass

Above right: The same sedums in autumn. Photo by Ed Snodgrass

Right: Mixed sedums, with *Sedum album* in flower. Photo by Nigel Dunnett

Above left: Prickly pear cactus (*Opuntia*), here growing on a green roof in Italy, is a good green roof plant for arid climates. Photo by Emilio Ancaya, Living Roofs, Inc.

Above: *Delosperma cooperi*, with beautiful daisy flowers, with another succulent, *Orostachys boehmeri*. Photo by Nigel Dunnett

Sedum hispanicum. Sedum spurium has larger, flatter leaves and provides a visual contrast to the other types in a mixture. Other commonly used succulents include *Delosperma*, with bright colourful flowers, although many are not frost tolerant, and low-growing cacti such as *Opuntia*.

Sedums have come to have a rather negative association on ecological and biodiversity grounds. This is to some extent unfounded and has more to do with the way they are used, rather than with the plants themselves. Sedum-only mats used in super-lightweight green roofs with little or no substrate will result in low-diversity roofs, sometimes with sparse or poor plant growth. However, when used in substrate-based systems and mixed with a wider diversity of plants, sedums can serve as an essential fail-safe component against summer drought and provide an excellent nectar source during the summer flowering period.

Flowering herbaceous species and alpines

Herbaceous and alpine plants give visual, structural, and ecological diversity to a green roof. Widely used and reliable species include tunic plant (*Petrorhagia saxifraga*), with pink flowers on dense, finely leaved plants, and chives (*Allium schoenoprasum*). *Dianthus* species such as *Dianthus deltoides* and *Dianthus carthusianorum* are effective, the latter seeding freely around a roof from year to year.

Above left: *Petrorhagia saxifraga* growing en masse from seed on a green roof, with *Dianthus carthusianorum* emerging. Photo by Green Estate Ltd.

Above: Golden thymes keep their bright appearance right through the winter. Photo by Nigel Dunnett

Left: In humid tropical climates, a very different range of green roof plants can be used. This pavilion at the Singapore Botanical Gardens is covered in ferns. Photo by Ben Nicholson

Grasses

Grasses can form the sole component of green roof vegetation, but on their own grasses can be prone to drought damage and die-back on unirrigated green roofs. As part of mixed vegetation, grasses provide visual contrast and additional structural diversity. Freely seeding grasses can dominate a roof and thus lower vegetation diversity. *Koeleria glauca* and *Koeleria macrantha* are suitable, as are many *Festuca* species.

Above: A grass roof in a small space. Photo by Nigel Dunnett

Top left: Unirrigated grass roofs dry out and ripen in the summer. Photo by Nigel Dunnett

Left: A simple turf roof. Photo by Wendy Allen

Native wildflowers

The increasing focus on green roofs for biodiversity has led to great interest in the use of native plant species. Every region in the world will have natural habitats containing species suitable for green roofs. In temperate climates, dry grassland plant communities are a good source of possible plants, with calcareous grasslands (chalk and limestone) being particularly suitable. Native species might be used on green roofs in two ways. Some natives may be substituted for non-natives, as part of a conventional planting mix, or more of a habitat creation or restoration ecology approach may be used, whereby an attempt is made to recreate a particular plant community. For example, reliable northern European species include cowslip (*Primula veris*), yarrow (*Achillea millefolium*), wild thyme (*Thymus drucei*), bird's foot trefoil (*Lotus corniculatus*), rough hawkbit (*Leontodon hispidus*), wall germander (*Teuchrium chamaedrys*), and sea campion (*Silene uniflora*).

Top: Limestone grasslands grow in very thin, poor, dry soils over pure rock. These conditions can be mimicked on a green roof. Photo by Nigel Dunnett

Above: Bird's foot trefoil (*Lotus corniculatus*). Photo by Nigel Dunnett

Right: Trials of native New Zealand plants for green roofs on small sheds. The species have a very exotic appearance compared with northern and western European green roof plants. Photo by Robyn Simcock

Bulbs

Smaller bulbs are invaluable in providing bright colourful highlights on a green roof. Bulbs which come from rocky desert environments, such as *Tulipa* species, are pre-adapted to withstanding summer heat and drought in very stony soils. Grape hyacinths (*Muscari*) are very reliable, as are dwarf *Narcissus*. In this area, there is still much research to be done on what will and won't work.

Above: Purple tulips on mounded substrate in a grassy green roof in Sheffield, United Kingdom. Photo by Nigel Dunnett

Left: Blue grape hyacinths (*Muscari*) with a red form of pasque flower (*Pulsatilla vulgaris*) and yellow cowslip (*Primula veris*). Photo by Nigel Dunnett

Annuals

Annual plants grow, flower, and set seed within a single growing season. They provide a burst of spring and summer colour, and many will seed themselves from year to year, filling gaps and popping up unexpectedly. Desert annuals and those from Mediterranean climates are particularly successful on green roofs. Species which prove reliable include sweet alyssum (*Alyssum maritimum*), which has strongly honey-scented white flowers and will carpet the ground. Tickseed (*Coreopsis tinctoria*) will thrive on a green roof, provided the soil is not too shallow. Fairy toadflax (*Linaria maroccana*) flowers very quickly and is good for providing quick colour while more slowly growing species or perennials become established. At a small scale, there is nothing to lose by scattering a few seeds of whatever comes to hand—some will work and some will not.

Below: A colourful mix of native cornfield annuals on a garage roof. Photo by Green Estate Ltd.

Below right: Pot marigolds (*Calendula*) among other annuals on a shed green roof. Photo by Emilio Ancaya, Living Roofs, Inc.

Moss

Moss comes naturally onto most roofs in most regions that are not arid, and it will commonly colonize very thin or poorly draining green roofs, where it can be seen as a sign of a very stressed or unhealthy roof. However, moss is extremely lightweight and will also absorb copious amounts of water. There have been proposals to exploit the value of moss in situations where anything else would create too much weight, using the old technique that gardeners employ to make new stone appear very old—painting a slurry containing milk or yoghurt onto the surface to encourage moss colonization.

Growing Vegetables and Herbs on the Roof

In crowded, high-density urban environments, interest is turning to using rooftops to grow food. Many typical aromatic culinary herbs come from Mediterranean climates and are very suitable for green roofs, provided the substrate is free-draining. Thymes, chives, oregano, rosemary, and lavender, for example, are frequently grown in green roofs.

This Japanese-style moss roof will only succeed in wetter climates or in shade. Photo by Wendy Allen

Growing more conventional crops requires more manipulation of the environment. Irrigation is certainly a requirement, substrate depth needs to be sufficient, and maintenance will certainly be great. The Eagle Street Rooftop Farms is an inspiring example of how a DIY mentality and active community and volunteer input can make this happen in an inner-city environment, even though the project is large in scale and a commercial build-up had to be used. At the opposite end of the scale, the Wheeler Street Leangreen House illustrates how food can be grown in a very small domestic space. The roof both provides a space for growing vegetables and fruits, and, as a cat- and slug-free space, is an ideal starting point for vegetable seedlings to be planted in the garden below. The Greensgrow Farms project illustrates hydroponics as a growing technique where there is no cultivatable soil. The topic of growing food at rooftop level is still very experimental, and the people doing it are pioneers. There is much still to be learned.

Vegetables growing on the rooftop farm at Eagle Street, Brooklyn. Photo by Annie Novak

Planting Styles

The way that plants are arranged and used on a roof is a matter of personal choice, and the design possibilities are wide. Opportunities range from the use of simple monocultures through to complex naturalistic mixtures. Green roofs don't have to be naturalistic: plants can be used in bold blocks and patterns.

Simple mixtures and monocultures

Extensive green roof planting is commonly done in simple mixtures and monocultures. The sedum roof is the most familiar example. Although often described as a monoculture, this is not technically correct because such roofs often contain several *Sedum* species giving rise to a range of textures and leaf and flower colours. The other familiar example is the grass, sod, or turf roof, although over time grass-only roofs can evolve into more species-rich communities.

These seemingly simple roofs can involve relatively high maintenance if the original vegetation is desired to be retained indefinitely. Almost inevitably, sedum-only roofs will be invaded by other types of plants. Should these be removed, or should we let nature take its course? Grassy monocultures usually require irrigation to stay green, or they brown off in summer or winter depending on your region.

Visually, simple low-diversity roofs tend to be rather monotonous or two dimensional. At the small scale, or where roofs are very visible or accessible, people tend to want a bit more aesthetic variety, textural contrast, and seasonal highlights, as well as a wider range of feeding opportunities for wildlife.

Patterns, blocks, and drifts

Planting in patterns is another design alternative. Groups, drifts, or sweeps of plants can create a visually exciting roof. Each group may be of a single species, or the drifts and masses can be of different vegetation types or mixtures, perhaps related to drifts and masses of varying substrate types on the roof.

Again, this is not a maintenance-free approach. Maintaining the

Mixed sedums. Photo by Nigel Dunnett

desired patterns may require a lot of intervention to stop one group mingling with another or to remove invading species. On the other hand, for many people, the development of a roof over time is one of the pleasures of having a green roof, and the breaking down and disintegration of patterns is a fascinating process.

Complex mixtures

Grouping plants in more complex mixtures is a good means of achieving a visually satisfying end point with relatively low maintenance requirements. Plants can be distributed singly or in small groups of the same species relatively randomly across the roof surface. Of course, this is what happens anyway if a roof is seeded, but the same naturalistic and spontaneous effect can be obtained through planting. At the simplest level, this may involve mixing plants with contrasting foliage or form among low-growing sedums, using chives, grasses, or drought-tolerant wildflower species, for example. It may involve more studied combination of plant forms, colours, and textures. Or it may be a random mix of species

Three different *Sedum* species growing in separate drifts provide fantastic contrasts in colour and texture. Photo by Nigel Dunnett

Above: This roof was planted by randomly distributing small groups of different species across the roof. Maintenance is much easier than if each species had to be kept distinct in separate larger drifts or clumps. Photo by Nigel Dunnett

Left: This random mix of sedums and perennials has pleasing contrasts in texture. Photo by Emilio Ancaya, Living Roofs, Inc.

chosen for their wildlife value or because they are members of a particular native plant community. Maintenance of mixtures can be a relatively simple affair, tweaking here and there to prevent the dominance of any one species.

Meadows

Meadows are a particular type of complex mixture. Green roofs are well suited to making wildflower meadows, because the difficult growing conditions tend to keep out the very vigorous grasses that outcompete the desirable wildflowers. Meadows can be created easily from seed. For a flower-rich effect, it is best not to include grasses at the outset or to include them only in small amounts. Grasses will come in anyway. By not using grasses initially in high density, the flowering plants have a greater chance to establish.

Plant Establishment Methods

Several options are available for vegetating a green roof, including pregrown vegetation mats, plug planting, cuttings, seeding, and natural colonization. There is no need to be restricted to using one method only. For example, plug plants can be used to create reliable and known vegetation at low density, with a seed mix sown between to create a greater vegetation cover at lower cost. Natural colonization can be enhanced by sowing and planting of desired species onto biodiverse roofs. Pregrown vegetated mats can also be oversown.

Pregrown vegetation mats

Vegetation mats offer instant greening to a known specification, and in some instances this may be the only option available. In these systems, a geotextile mat supports a thin layer of growing medium, into which the plants are established at the plant nursery. The mats are transported, either flat or rolled up, to the green roof site. By far the most common type is sedum mats, composed of a mix of different *Sedum* species. Very often such mats are laid over minimal depths of substrate or directly onto a moisture retention mat, thereby creating a very lightweight system.

Above: A green roof meadow in Sheffield, with yellow *Anthemis tinctoria*. Photo by Nigel Dunnett

Left: A beautiful green roof meadow with *Dianthus carthusianorum*. Wildflower meadows on green roofs can be very successful because the stressful conditions keep out dominant and vigorous grasses. Photo by APP Dachgarten GmbH

Good contact between the vegetation mat and whatever is underneath is essential during the establish phase, and irrigation may be necessary.

Species-diverse vegetation mats are also available for green roofs. These include a range of flowering plants and may or may not contain sedums. Such mats have greater aesthetic appeal and biodiversity value, but must be used with a substrate layer.

Traditional turf may also be used to create instant vegetation cover. Wildflower turf can contain a good range of appropriate native species. However, the use of turf on a green roof should only be considered where irrigation is available for establishment and a reasonable depth of growing medium is being used.

Given the long-term nature of green roofs, instant complete vegetation cover is not necessary for effective functioning, unless it is essential for aesthetic or practical purposes, such as when a limited time is available for vegetation establishment. The following methods require a longer establishment time, but they are generally less expensive options than pregrown mats.

Green roofs on houses and storage sheds created with a pregrown sedum mat. Photo by Nigel Dunnett

Plug planting

Plugs are small rooted cuttings or seedlings grown in cell trays containing compost. They are relatively inexpensive and allow a roof to be vegetated with a known mix of plants in the desired densities and arrangements. The plugs are planted directly into the substrate spread on the roof. The typical density of planting is ten to fifteen plants per square metre. Planting in staggered rows ensures a more even coverage. The plugs should not be allowed to dry out in the trays and should be thoroughly moistened before planting—dry plugs will hinder or prevent root outgrowth into the surrounding green roof medium—and the roof kept moist until the plug plants begin to root out into the growing medium. *Sedum* species are also available in larger plugs or discs which are established in exactly the same manner.

In some instances, desired plants may not be available as plug plants, and container-grown plants may have to be used. The smallest container size possible should be used, because the mass of highly organic compost in most nursery container plants can hinder new root growth out into the harsher green roof growing medium. If container plants are to be used, the roots should be loosened prior to planting to enable the greatest contact of roots with the green roof medium.

Top right: Green roof vegetation created using a species-rich pregrown mat by Lindum Turf of North Yorkshire. Photo by Nigel Dunnett

Right: Trays of green roof plug plants in production. Purple-flowered *Talinum calycinum* is a beautiful annual or short-lived perennial. Photo by Nigel Dunnett

Cuttings

Sedum species root readily from fragments of leaves and stems. Bags of sedum cuttings are readily available, and these are strewn across the surface of the levelled growing medium on the roof. It is essential that the cuttings remain moist until rooting has occurred. On a large scale, hydro-seeding techniques are used, whereby the cuttings are pumped out onto the roof in a slurry of water-retentive gel and nutrients. The additional moisture-holding capacity of the gel aids establishment.

Seeding

Seeding as an establishment technique on green roofs has been underused to date, but it is likely to feature more prominently in the future. It is a relatively inexpensive method, and the use of a seed mix across an entire roof surface enables different component species to find the conditions that suit them best. However, the precise composition of the vegetation cannot be guaranteed because of the variability of germination of species from year to year and site to site.

Below: A tray of *Sedum reflexum* plugs. Photo by Nigel Dunnett

Below right: A green roof newly planted with plug plants. Photo by Green Estate Ltd.

Seeding is undertaken on to the bare growing medium surface. If the roof has been standing unvegetated for some time, it will be necessary to loosen or lightly cultivate the surface and remove any unwanted seedlings. Because quantities of seed are small (for example, 3–4 g/m² [0.1 oz/sq yd] for grass seed, 5–8 g/m² [0.2 oz/sq yd] for wildflowers only), the seed is often mixed with a bulking agent, such as sand or sawdust, to enable even spreading. The growing medium should be moist prior to sowing. After sowing, the seed should be lightly raked and firmed into the surface. The roof should be kept moist during dry periods, and ideally, the area covered with netting to keep birds off the surface.

An alternative approach that is particularly useful if the growing medium is very coarse and seeds are likely to fall or be washed deep into the substrate is to spread a thin layer of sand or fine growing medium containing the required seed mix over the surface. The seed will already be incorporated well into the growing medium, and therefore the surface will only require a light firming.

Seeding is best undertaken in the autumn or in late winter and spring.

This green roof in Sheffield, United Kingdom, was created by sowing the same seed mix over the entire roof. Slight differences in substrate depth across the roof have resulted in differences in the vegetation. Photo by Nigel Dunnett

The dry hot summer months should be avoided. Some species require winter chilling, and therefore spring sowing of the plants would not be effective.

Natural colonization

The most cost-effective and ecological approach to vegetating green roofs is to allow natural colonization, enabling plants which blow on to the roof surface naturally or are brought there by birds to establish unaided. This is a good technique for vegetating biodiverse roofs. Those plants which establish, survive, and persist will be, by definition, well-adapted to the green roof conditions and will also be reflective of the typical vegetation of disturbed sites in the immediate area. This approach is best used with infertile or free-draining substrate, because rich and productive substrates can encourage a rank, low-diversity outcome. However, natural colonization leaves very little control over the composition of the vegetation, and only certain types of plants are able to get to the roof (for example, those which are dispersed easily by wind). Many of the really tough and reliable

The purple toadflax (*Linaria purpurea*) on this green roof in Sheffield, United Kingdom, colonized the roof naturally. Photo by Nigel Dunnett

green roof plants are not so mobile and would never get to the roof by these means. Because of the lack of control over the vegetation and the type of plants that arrive easily, the aesthetic appearance can be very wild. Conversely, some very interesting and unexpected species can arrive, creating a unique and distinctive roof.

Maintenance

The prospect of having to commit to ongoing maintenance of a green roof in what might be a difficult and inaccessible situation can be one of the things that puts people off having a green roof. But in reality, the amount of maintenance required can be relatively slight or almost non-existent. One of the key factors in minimizing maintenance is to get the substrate right. A low-nutrient, free-draining substrate is going to cause much less of a weed problem compared to a highly organic and nutrient-rich material.

There is a common fallacy that green or grassy roofs need to be mown or grazed. In reality, roofs probably do not need any cutting back—the dried-out flower heads and stalks make a good silhouette against the sky in the winter and may be good sources of seed and shelter for birds and invertebrates.

Vigorous woody plants, such as tree and shrub seedlings, should be removed from a green roof. Not only may the roots present a problem to the underlying layers of the roof, but, if they reach any size, they are liable to be blown over, thereby pulling up the surrounding substrate and vegetation.

With time, a green roof may become very low in nutrients, and there may be a need for the more horticulturally inclined roofs to be given a top-up—either with an organic slow-release fertilizer or by top-dressing with compost or additional substrate.

Of course, we assume that maintenance is always something to be avoided, but for many people who have their own small-scale green roof, tinkering around with it and keeping it looking good is part of the pleasure. Green roofs can be gardened to whatever level of intensity you are prepared to put in.

GREEN ROOFS AND BIODIVERSITY

ANY GREEN roof is going to be of some value for wildlife. However, it is possible to design in plants and features that create a unique and diverse habitat at roof level. Although much of research in this area has been conducted mainly in Europe, the principles will apply wherever a small green roof is to be constructed.

Extensive green roofs are generally low in nutrients and well drained. These characteristics are of particular importance for a wide range of interesting plants and invertebrate fauna. Certainly in Europe this type of habitat is becoming increasingly rare as the intensification of agriculture is causing old meadows and unimproved grasslands to be ploughed up and destroyed. These old grassland were very rich in plant diversity and supported a wide range of invertebrates and birds. But now in the United Kingdom, for example, many of the species associated with these types of habitats are mainly found on postindustrial sites that have been left to nature to colonize. These brownfield sites, which most people think of as demolition sites, wasteland, or derelict land, are often very rich in wildlife. Such sites are often covered in layers of broken and crushed bricks and concrete, all of which is free-draining and ideal for the development of diverse vegetation. Piles of abandoned materials provide many opportunities for invertebrates to find shelter, and areas of poor drainage give rise to miniature wetlands. Because brownfield sites are seen as derelict, few people go on to them, so wildlife is left undisturbed. And yet these sites are increasingly being targeted for new developments.

Extensive green roofs offer an opportunity for such flora and fauna to relocate onto roofs, and even small green roofs can offer a refuge for these species. When building a green roof, however, there is an opportunity to create a range of microhabitats to ensure that as wide a range of flora and fauna can take refuge at the roof level. Depending on your approach, a green roof can also provide a unique opportunity to allow an area of untidiness within a property.

There are several basic principles when designing for wildlife. These

The flower-rich vegetation is perfect for the honey bees in this hive on a London green roof. Photo by Dusty Gedge

principles are based on research carried out in the last ten years on large-scale green roofs in London and Switzerland, but they are easily transferable to small-scale roofs. More recently, similar research in the United States has demonstrated exactly the same wildlife benefits of green roofs.

Basic Design Principles

Virtually any green roof will attract some wildlife, but to maximize the opportunities for attracting the widest range of invertebrates and plants it is necessary to widen the diversity of ecological conditions on the roof. The guidelines that follow indicate how this can be done, but there is no strict design form or style that has to be followed. Green roofs for wildlife don't have to be wild, and the shapes and patterns don't have to be free-form. All these principles can be just as easily applied in a more formal or geometric layout or in more organic patterns.

Vary the depth of the substrate

Varying the depth of the growing medium, preferably between 50 and 150 mm (2–6 in), will allow for a range of microhabitats and growing

Postindustrial urban sites can be wildlife havens. The variety of materials, landforms, and drainage can support diverse communities of plants, invertebrates, and birds. Photo by Nigel Dunnett

conditions, providing both dry conditions with sparsely vegetated areas and more lush areas of taller vegetation. The effect of the varied substrate will also provide slopes for a range of burrowing invertebrates to find opportunities to nest. Mounding also creates differences in aspect and sun and shade, providing an even wider array of ecological conditions.

Use different substrates

Different substrates, including rubble and stony material, sand, and brick-based or similar media, provide different opportunities for invertebrates. Rubble and stony areas offer shelter and nesting opportunities for certain species. Sandy areas and commercial brick-based substrates and media will allow burrowing bees and other invertebrates to have nesting opportunities.

Provide a diversity of plants

Having a wide array of plant species will allow a range of invertebrate species to colonize the roof. Consideration should be given to plants that provide both nectar and food for butterflies, moths, and their caterpillars. Research in Switzerland has shown that roofs that are planted with a range of herbs, grasses, and sedums provide a foraging source for a wide range of wildlife throughout the season. Sedum-only roofs attracted bees for a short period when the plants were in flower in June and July. Therefore, it is good to consider plants that flower in early spring and late summer to ensure that the roof provides the best possible resource for nectar-feeding fauna. Plant diversity also increases the sheltering and habitat opportunities for invertebrates. A mix of low-growing species, grasses, and plants with upright flowering stems may encourage a greater range of spiders and beetles, for example, than simple vegetation with no structural diversity. This may also increase the chances of some invertebrates being able to survive over winter in hollow dried grass stalks, for example.

Use a diversity of plants and different plant establishment methods

There is always a dilemma between wanting an instant effect and allowing a roof to develop into what it wants to be. Enabling a roof to evolve,

NATURE ROOFS

Whether you are someone with a distinct interest in nature, a designer, or a gardener, a small green roof can offer a unique oasis within the footprint of a garden or building plot. Due to the nature of extensive green roofs, a range of species that would not otherwise be able to reside in a well-tended garden can be attracted to the dry conditions on a roof. Such an approach can provide an important and interesting landscape of plants, logs, stones, old rope, or other objects that take your fancy to give added pleasure to whoever looks out onto the roof and provide a valuable resource for nature. Most of this may well escape the eye but will ensure that your roof is a complex, diverse, and dynamic micro ecosystem.

The opportunities for creative design are endless. Nature roofs can be wild and random in appearance or can be highly structured. Logs and stones and other materials can be arranged in patterns, and the use of different substrates, which may have very different textures and colours, can produce striking visual results.

however, will mean that the vegetation that develops is totally adapted to that particular roof. Waiting for this to take place can provide an element of anticipation. From a wildlife perspective, the different planting methods have their benefits. For example, plug planting will provide some immediate interest for wildlife. Seeding a range of appropriate species, especially on roofs with a varied substrate depth and type, will allow the plants to establish themselves where they want to be. Bulbs will supply an early source of nectar, and annuals can provide an instant effect and are a good source of nectar in the first year.

Provide other structural features

Using logs and stones or boulders can add another dimension to a small-scale green roof. Not only do such structural features offer habitat and an opportunity to create some interesting designs, they also provide plants with some shade and protection from the wind. Certain plants that may struggle on extensive roofs could be planted on the leeward shady side of such features. A European example is common toadflax (*Linaria vulgaris*), which does not grow well in 100 mm (4 in) of substrate on green roofs. We have found that when planted between two logs it will actually thrive, most probably because the logs create a slightly moister environment which tends to dries out less. Adding invertebrate nesting boxes and small sand walls for mining bees can provide further nesting opportunities.

While green roofs will often attract species in passing, it is more difficult to establish viable breeding populations—this has been noted especially for birds. Young birds, in particular, need water sources for drinking. It is feasible to design in small areas of open water on a green roof, if loading requirements will allow. However, maintaining shallow areas of water can be very difficult on a roof because high temperatures and wind create ideal conditions for evaporation.

Relate to your local area

Each region has its own distinctive native habitats and plant and animal communities, which are usually strongly related to climate and to geology. A major objective of creating green roofs for biodiversity is to attract and draw in wildlife from the surrounding area. Using native plants can

Top left: Green roofs for wildlife can have strong design content. This example, prior to planting and colonization by plants, uses repeated patterns of substrate materials and logs. Photo by Dusty Gedge

Left: This green roof on the Laban Dance Centre, London, has a diverse mix of plants as well as open, sunny, stony places, giving rise to a mosaic of conditions across the roof. Photo by Dusty Gedge

Above: This green roof on top of the Barclays building in London has an open, stony surface. Photo by Dusty Gedge

help to achieve this, particularly because in some cases insect larvae will only eat a particular species and no other, and local pollinating insects may also be linked with native plant species. The use of regionally native vegetation can help replace lost habitat. In some regions, non-native plants with invasive tendencies have become a major problem, and using native species avoids the danger of introducing such potential problem plants.

There are other, less ecological reasons for relating a green roof to the locality. A sense of local distinctiveness and connection to place makes a stand against the relentless uniformity and homogenization of our built environment, and using locally derived soils and substrate materials can be a lot cheaper than buying in ready-made growing media. Therefore, consider where you are and what substrates, growing media, and plant species will replicate the characteristics of your local area. The green roof on Georgina Cape's garage is a good example of this principle.

Wildlife on Green Roofs

There are a lot of opportunities for wildlife to forage and nest on a small green roof, although much of it will be on the micro scale. The diversity of invertebrate species is a good indicator of the ecological health of a green roof. Research on biodiversity has generally focused on certain families and orders, notably spiders, beetles, and the Hymenoptera (bees, wasps, and ants). These species are very mobile and colonize green roofs easily, but, of course, many other animals also will be attracted to green roofs and will colonize from some distance.

Spiders

Spiders are particularly good indicators of the habitat quality of a green roof. Being the ultimate invertebrate predator, they are at the pinnacle of the invertebrate food chain. Therefore, the range of spider species is indicative of the total invertebrate diversity of a green roof. Although spiders are not so dependent on specific vegetation, for some species the height of the vegetation influences whether they will colonize a green roof. Some species are thermophilic (they need warmer conditions) and prefer very open, sparsely vegetated microhabitats, whereas others, especially those that create webs, prefer areas of taller, structural vegetation. Spiders quickly colonize roofs as most throw out a thin thread and are blown about by the wind until they come to rest.

Some rare spiders have been found on roofs in London, including the wolf spider *Pardosa agrestis* and *Philodromus albidus*. The very rare *Zodarion italicum* has even made it 160 m (535 ft) onto a tower block in London. However, common species are important as well. Over 26 percent of U.K. spider species were found on green roofs in the London area. For example, *Xysticus cristatus* is a common crab spider found on sedum roofs.

The crab spider *Xysticus cristatus* inhabits sedum green roofs. Photo by Dave Perkins

Beetles

Beetles are both carnivorous and herbivorous. A lot of rare beetles are associated with specific plant species, and therefore a green roof with a very diverse beetle fauna will reflect the quality of the vegetation as wildlife habitat. Like spiders, beetles fall into two categories: some are thermophilic and prefer open, sparsely vegetated habitat, whereas others need more structural diversity.

A good example of a beetle associated with a specific plant is *Olibrus flavicornis*, a rare U.K. ground beetle associated with autumn hawkbit (*Leontodon autumnalis*), a good extensive green roof plant. This particular beetle is a priority species in the London Olympics Biodiversity Action Plan and can be found on small green roofs which have been planted or seeded with the host plant.

Other interesting and rare beetles that have been discovered on roofs in London include the patio beetle (*Tachys parvulus*), which is found on very stressed sedum blanket roofs. The Adonis ladybird (*Hippodamia variegata*) has even been found on a green roof 160 m (535 ft) high.

Hymenoptera

The order Hymenoptera includes the solitary and social bees, wasps, and ants. The presence of a range of species throughout the year will suggest that both substrate types and depths are providing nesting opportunities and that there is a good range of plant species for various hymenopterans and their individual needs. Such insects can be actively encouraged through use of bee hotels, insect nest boxes, and mason bee blocks. Such structures are readily available from garden centres, but blocks of wood drilled with holes and bundles of straws, canes, and other hollow material can equally suffice.

When selecting plants for a green roof, include a range of species that allows both long-tongued and short-tongued bumble bees (*Bombus*) to feed. Furthermore, many species of Hymenoptera require particular characteristics in the growing medium to allow them to nest—it must be soft and easy to burrow into, without being prone to collapse, such as sand and soft earth. Spring bulbs on roofs not only provide an early nectar source, but we have noticed that early mining bees (*Andrena haemorrhoa*) make their nests at the base of *Tulipa linifolia* and *Muscari armeniacum* 'Cantab' bulbs and then use these flowers as beacons to guide them back to their nests.

The widespread reduction in bee numbers has raised concern recently, and, apart from disease, this decline has largely been attributed to loss of habitat in the wild. Urban areas are becoming increasingly important in supporting bee populations, and rooftops in particular have great

Bumble bees on viper's bugloss (*Echium vulgare*). Photo by Dusty Gedge

potential as unused spaces that are generally away from people. A large number of bee species have been observed both in Switzerland and in London using green roofs, including the brown carder bee (*Bombus pascuorum*), buff tailed bumble bee (*Bombus terrestris*), white tailed bumble bee (*Bombus lucorum*), wool carder bee (*Anthidium manicatum*), Gwynne's mining bee (*Andrena bicolor*), cuckoo bee (*Nomada fabriciana*), patchwork leaf cutter bee (*Megachile centuncularis*), and spider hunting wasp (*Anoplius viaticus*).

Butterflies and moths

Adult butterflies and moths will of course use a green roof if it has a good source of nectar. As important, though, is the presence of food plants that their caterpillars need to develop into the adult stage. Selecting plants that are known hosts for moths and butterflies will increase the diversity of the roof and bring these beautiful insects to your roof. For example, the San Francisco Academy of Science green roof included extensive planting of dwarf plantain (*Plantago erecta*) to provide food for the caterpillars of the bay checkerspot butterfly (*Euphydryas editha bayensis*). In London a number of butterfly and moth species have been seen flying over green roofs, including the red admiral (*Vanessa atalanta*), painted lady (*Vanessa cardui*), small tortoiseshell (*Aglais urticae*), Burnet companion moth (*Euclidia glyphica*), and carnation tortrix (*Cacoecimorpha pronubana*). Several species and their caterpillars have been seen on roofs, including the rare toadflax brocade (*Calophasia lunula*), the caterpillars of which feed on *Linaria vulgaris*, six-spotted Burnet moth (*Zygaena filipendulae*), the larvae of which feed on *Lotus corniculatus*, and the small blue butterfly (*Cupido minimus*), which feeds on *Anthyllis vulneraria*. In a Sheffield study that investigated the influence of height of green roof on the presence of butterflies and honey bees, butterflies tended to be found on only the lower level roofs, while honey bees were found at all levels.

Birds

Birds of various kinds will be attracted to a small green roof, although not always for the good. Some common garden birds will pluck out plugs shortly after planting, when the roots are not well established. Pigeons

The burnet companion moth (*Euclidia glyphica*) on kidney vetch on a green roof. Photo by Dusty Gedge

will dust-bathe in areas of open substrate and eat freshly sown seeds. Crows can pick up and drop stones and pebbles. All of which can be a little irritating and completely unwelcome.

However, a well-established small green roof, depending on the plant species, will attract a wide range of bird species. Where plants with good seed heads have been established, finches will come to feed from the flower heads. Goldfinches (*Carduelis carduelis*) feed on the flower heads of plants including teasels (*Dipsacus sylvestris*) and viper's bugloss (*Echium vulgare*). House sparrows (*Passer domesticus*) are commonly seen on roofs with good grass and herbs. Common vetch (*Vicia sativa*) seems to be particularly important for house sparrows as it tends to attract a profusion of aphids, an important food for young house sparrow chicks (as well as for ladybird beetles). A word of warning, however: this particular plant can start to take over a roof if the soil is slightly nutrient rich.

Other bird species are attracted to green roofs in general, but they are dependent on the size and location of a given green roof. It is highly unlikely that small-scale green roofs would attract ground-nesting bird species such as larks or plovers, but certainly in the United Kingdom and mainland Europe small roofs are likely to attract the black redstart (*Phoenicurus ochruros*).

Birds such as plovers may nest on large green roofs, but smaller green roofs are only likely to attract birds for feeding visits. Photo by Ed Snodgrass

GREEN ROOFS
on Sheds, Garden Offices, and Studios

Nigel Dunnett's garden sheds in Sheffield, United Kingdom. Photo by Nigel Dunnett

DUNNETT GARDEN SHED

Crosspool, Sheffield, United Kingdom • Owner and designer: **Nigel Dunnett**
• Context: **Garden shed** • Size: **3 x 4 m (9 x 12 ft)** • Main purpose of
green roof: **Aesthetic, horticulture, biodiversity, food growing, experimental**

THIS SHED in my garden was largely responsible
for my initial interest in green roofs—an interest
which has developed subsequently into a major part
of my life. In 1999 I moved into a new house on a
steeply sloping hillside in Sheffield. Although the
house faced onto a normal urban street, behind the
house there had been no development because of the
slope, and the relatively small garden backed onto
open fields. A large area of the garden was taken up
by a substantial garden shed and store. Because the
garden sloped downwards, the grey felted roof of
the shed was very visible from the house. I had the
option of removing the shed, but the storage space
was very useful. I knew what green roofs were, having seen them during visits to Germany, but had
little or no idea how they worked or what they were
made from. However, as a professional ecologist, I
was intrigued. Instead of demolishing the shed, I
decided to use it as an opportunity to try and make
a green roof of my own, one that would beautify an

The living wall of Nigel Dunnett's shed contains many
alpines, planted into gaps in the dry stone. Photo by Nigel
Dunnett

ugly structure and integrate it both into the garden and with the fields beyond.

At the time, the idea of green roofs at the small garden scale was unheard of—all the examples were large scale. It seemed that in the United Kingdom, the rooftop was just about the only area in gardens that had not been exploited for plant growing. I saw it as the final horticultural frontier.

Designing and planning

The existing building appeared relatively sturdy. The roof joists were new, the rest of the building was old, and there were signs of decay in the plywood walls. It was questionable as to whether the building would support significant loading. Although I am happy to take on any sort of garden work involving plants, I am the first to admit that I have no DIY skills or inclination whatsoever. At the time I would not have

known where to start in terms of strengthening the roof or the building. The best solution for me, therefore, was to build an external shell around the building and to use this to support a new roof platform. This had the added benefit of enabling me to make new cladding for the walls of the building. In effect, the old shed was enclosed in a new, living skin. I had no drawn plan for the building—more of a vision in my head. The final form of the building evolved over the two years it took me to make it in my spare time.

Installation

I sunk four 100 × 100 mm (4 × 4 in) posts at each corner of the shed, with their tops 100 mm (4 in) below the level of the existing roof surface. I then placed horizontal 100 × 100 mm (4 × 4 in) beams onto these, making a framework around the whole perimeter of the roof, at roof level, with supporting

consisted of a mix of materials that I could get hold of at the time. LECA (expanded clay) and crushed brick were mixed with a proprietary soil-based gritty garden compost (John Innes no. 3). The roof was planted with sedums (*Sedum acre, Sedum reflexum,* and *Sedum album*), *Dianthus carthusianorum,* chives (*Allium schoenoprasum*), *Petrorhagia saxifraga, Thymus vulgaris,* sea thrift (*Armeria maritima*), *Erodium manescavi,* wall germander (*Teuchrium chamaedrys*), hawkbit (*Leontodon hispidus*), and blue fescue grass (*Festuca glauca*). Plants were watered on establishment, but then subsequently the roof received no irrigation. No maintenance was carried out—those species best adapted survived, and others were allowed to freely seed themselves in.

The roof was built with limited resources. I initially spread substrate and planted only the 1-m (3-ft) perimeter of the roof, with the intention of filling in the rest as funds allowed. In the end, the whole of the roof was not filled in. However, unless you physically climbed up onto the roof, this would not be apparent—from ground level and from the house, only the edge could be seen, and unless specially told, people automatically assumed the whole roof

75 × 75 mm (3 × 3 in) supporting posts placed regularly around the roof at 1-m (3-ft) intervals. Next 75 × 75 mm (3 × 3 in) joists were then laid across these beams in one direction, 450 mm (18 in) apart, and sheets of exterior plywood were then fixed to these to make a level surface. I then laid butyl rubber pond liner over the whole surface. The whole roof sloped slightly backwards, so water could drain off the back end, directly onto the original felted roof surface of the old shed. I then simply tacked on some thin (150-mm, 6-in) planks around the edge to hide the structure and stop growing medium from falling off the roof. The supporting posts enabled me to tack on 75-mm (3-in) boards as new cladding at the front of the shed. All materials were from the local DIY centre. The whole structure was then painted.

The growing medium was spread directly onto the pond liner to a depth of 100–150 mm (4–6 in) and

The rooftop was just about the only area in gardens that had not been exploited for plant growing. I saw it as the final horticultural frontier.

had been planted. I never made any pretence that the roof was planted for any significant benefit beyond aesthetic, and therefore the perimeter planting more than achieved this objective.

At the side of the shed I created a living wall. I simply adhered a pond liner up against the existing wall surface as a waterproofing layer, and then built up dry-stone walling in front, using the upright posts at 1-m (3-ft) intervals as a framework, packing the stones in very tightly. A gap of 25–50 mm (1–2 in) was left between the stones and the wall. As I built up the wall, I packed the space behind with gritty compost, and inserted small plants (mostly cuttings and seedlings of plants from the green roof) into gaps in the stones as they arose, again packing in with compost. Water from the roof drains down behind the wall, providing irrigation after rain.

Success of the green roof

The green roof thrived, although the vegetation changed dramatically over time. The blue fescue grass is now dominant—it is a vigorous self-seeder. But this has resulted in a shimmering steely blue meadow. Some of the flowering plants have proved to be remarkably resilient within this meadow— *Sedum reflexum*, hawkbit, and particularly the chives and thyme have spread throughout. In fact, the roof became my main source of these herbs. Dandelions (*Taraxacum officinale*) have colonized, and another invader, the annual scentless mayweed (*Tripleurospermum maritimum*), flowers for most of the summer.

The creation of the green roof provided the impetus for the transformation of the complete shed.

The meadow roof makes a visual connection with the planting on the ground. Photo by Nigel Dunnett

From a former eyesore, the shed became an integral and essential part of the garden design. Moreover, having a visually prominent meadow on the rooftop made a strong visual link to the meadow and naturalistic planting that was found in the garden on the ground. I made no attempt at wonderful construction detailing or finishing, and everything is pretty rough and ready. But to me, somehow that adds to the appeal.

DUNNETT PREFAB SHED

Crosspool, Sheffield, United Kingdom • Owner and designer: **Nigel Dunnett** • Context: **Garden shed** • Size: **1 × 2.5 m (3 × 8 ft)** • Main purpose of green roof: **Aesthetic, horticulture, biodiversity, demonstration**

The shed in winter. Photo by Nigel Dunnett

IN SUMMER 2004, I went away for a week on a study tour and returned to find that we had acquired a second-hand shed from our neighbours. Although at first somewhat flabbergasted that we had yet another structure in what was already a very crowded garden, I quickly began to see this as another opportunity to make a green roof. The shed was typical of the sort that can be picked up from any garden centre or DIY store: a very thin timber structure, with a simple double-pitched roof of wooden slats, covered with roofing felt. I set myself the challenge of seeing if I could make a green roof on this shed, without any complicated structural support for the building, using only inexpensive materials and plants which would be available to anyone from their local garden centre or DIY store.

In so doing, I had another aim. For many people, the garden shed is something to be tucked out of sight at the end of the garden. I wanted to show how a green roof could be used to transform what is often regarded as an ugly structure into something

The completed shed.
Photo by Nigel Dunnett

of beauty, something that could take centre stage in a garden. I therefore resisted the temptation to put the shed at the very end of the garden. Instead I put it bang halfway in the middle, thereby creating two separate spaces—one in front, one behind. Moreover, I also avoided the temptation to place the shed square on in the garden, in line with a boundary. Instead, I placed it at an angle. Again, this created a new dynamic and enabled me to create views and sightlines with the shed as a focal point. The garden slopes downwards, and I set the shed slightly into the slope, so that the far side is at ground level, but by infilling in front of the shed, and making a small deck of old railway sleepers to this level, the ground at the front of the shed is around 450 mm (18 in) higher than at the back.

Designing and planning

At the time, there were few examples of green roofs on sheds or other garden buildings. I therefore was left with little choice but to try and work out how to do it myself. I freely admit to having little in the way of carpentry, building, or DIY skills or inclination, and had little idea at the time of how one might increase the loading capacity of shed by internal strengthening or support. I therefore looked to providing some external strengthening. As a gardener, I am much more comfortable making things in external space, rather than internal space. My approach was to create a wooden tray which sat on top of the existing roof surface. With my rudimentary understanding of physics, I felt that, although some of the loading of such a tray is imposed directly downwards

Left: A timber edge is held in place with external supports. Photo by Nigel Dunnett

Below: A timber tray sits on top of a waterproofing liner laid on top of the original surface. Photo by Nigel Dunnett

on to the roof surface, on a pitched roof, a proportion of the forces are also directed more horizontally, in effect trying to force the tray to slide off the roof. By placing retaining structures in front of the tray, some of the loading can be deflected into those structures.

Installation

I placed 75 × 75 mm (3 × 3 in) posts directly along the front edge of the shed, fixed in concrete and braced to the shed, with the top of the posts extending 100 mm (4 in) above the level of the front edge of the shed. A butyl rubber pond liner was draped over

---

With a new path to the shed and some judicious tree planting to frame the view, the pepped-up shed has become the focal point of the entire garden

---

the existing roof surface for additional waterproofing and root protection. A wooden framework of 150-mm (6-in) planks was then constructed to sit directly on the liner, with the front edge resting against the supporting posts. The framework divided the roof into smaller rectangular cells into which the growing medium was placed and which prevented slippage of the medium. Water drained directly under the framework. The growing medium was a 1:1 mix of LECA (expanded clay) and gritty John Innes no. 3 compost to a depth of 100–150 mm (4–6 in), over

a drainage layer of crushed aerated concrete breeze blocks. The plants were obtained from a variety of sources. Some were raised from seed, but the majority were alpines obtained as small plants from the local garden centre.

Success of the green roof

Species included the sedums in various coloured-leaved forms: *Sedum album, Sedum album* 'Coral Carpet', and *Sedum spurium*. A number of different thymes have been persistent, the most effective of which has been the golden-leaved *Thymus* 'Bertram Anderson', which is bright in both winter and summer. Sea campion (*Silene uniflora*) flowered very well for a few years but has subsequently died out. Low-growing *Dianthus* has proved to be persistent, as has harebell (*Campanula rotundifolia*). Alpine storksbills (*Erodium*) have been particularly effective, flowering for eight months of the year. *Penstemon pinifolius* 'Mersea Yellow', a refined relative of yarrow (*Achillea nobilis*), has been very successful. Grasses included the refined and graceful *Festuca amethystina* with purple-tinged flower stems.

The roof has received surprisingly little maintenance. The need for weeding is minimal because the growing medium is free-draining and has low fertility, and this does not appear to be good for weed establishment. The one exception has been white clover (*Trifolium repens*). A single plant became established and is spreading rapidly, and it is difficult to remove from among other plants. Being a nitrogen-fixing legume, white clover is able to fend for itself in stressful conditions. The roof has not been fertilized, but it does get water during very dry periods. The whole point is that it looks good, so I don't see

Diverse planting of alpines on the roof. Photo by Nigel Dunnett

much advantage in being highly principled about not giving a bit of water every now and again, especially as grey water from the house can be used on this very infrequent basis.

Having had more experience now, I would be more confident in strengthening a building from inside. However, the external supports did enable me to transform what was a flimsy looking structure into something that appeared to be much more substantial. By painting the whole shed black, and by adding simple wooden batons around the windows to give the appearance of proper window frames, the shed is unrecognizable from its former self. Having the small decked area raised up in front of the shed means that you can walk right up to the roof and see the plants. This, combined with a new path to the shed and some judicious tree planting to frame the view, means that the pepped-up shed has become the focal point of the entire garden.

The green roof in summer and autumn. Photos by JKLA Studio

North Tonawanda, New York, United States • Owner and designer: **Joy Kuebler Landscape Architect, PC** • Context: **Residential garage and office** • Size: **19 m² (200 sq ft)** • Main purpose of green roof: **Demonstration**

JOY IS A landscape architect in North Tonawanda, a small town between Buffalo and Niagara Falls, New York, adjacent to two of the Great Lakes. Her small company had outgrown its office space in the house, but from the perspective of her family life it was important that the office be on the property. Creating a new office in their garden gave them the opportunity to explore sustainable design on a residential scale in an area of the country still entrenched in traditional construction methods and materials.

Joy says, 'When we told people we were going to be building a green roof, people literally thought we were painting the roof with green paint!' When converting the garage to make the office, she and her colleagues felt the whole building project needed to be a living example of sustainable design and construction at a residential scale. For landscape architects, having a green roof was a great way to demonstrate that they were 'walking the walk and talking the talk' of sustainability. It allowed them an opportunity to really live with the roof, watch it develop, and report on its progress from a professional perspective. In western New York, Joy's company were having a difficult time getting people to understand the concept of a garden on the roof, and this would be a living, breathing example that people could see, touch, and study. 'As landscape architects, sustainability is something we incorporate into every project,' Joy notes, 'and the green roof was a way for us to become more familiar with a green roof system and to introduce this sustainable element in a way that was more approachable.'

Joy's first experience with green roofs was in Norway in 1990 as an exchange student. 'While I knew nothing of landscape architecture at the time, I was in awe of the sod roofs,' she says. Several years and an education in landscape architecture later, she came across an article in *This Old House* magazine highlighting simple green roofs on porches, garages, sheds, and summer houses. After several more years, she decided to move forward on the garage construction and knew a green roof had to be a part of the project.

The green roof is on a former garage in the garden of the house, which is in a typical residential neighbourhood. The green roof faces south, and a traditional asphalt shingle roof on the building faces north. The roof is 5.4 m (18 ft) off the ground and is on a steep (7:12, 30°) slope. Because the original 1948 garage was constructed without foundations or a floor, the family had never used it as a place for the car. The idea of living without a dedicated storage area for the car was something they were already used to.

Designing and planning

After some basic and preliminary research, Joy decided on an extensive roof with a maximum substrate depth of 12.5 cm (5 in). Because the Buffalo region has notoriously snowy winters, snow loading was already calculated into the structure, so adding an additional load for the green roof was not as significant as it might be in other climates.

Joy decided the south-facing side would be the green roof and the north face would be a traditional asphalt shingle roof. This was primarily for costing purposes, but she was also very intrigued about the

---

It allowed them an opportunity to really live with the roof, watch it develop, and report on its progress from a professional perspective.

---

idea of having a continuous experiment on hand. How did the two sides perform against each other? How much stormwater was collected from each side during any typical rainfall event? A unique ridge detail was constructed to bridge between the two surfaces and allow for the depth of the growing medium.

To allow for head room inside the structure and to be sure the height of the building did not exceed zoning conditions, the slope of the roof needed to be steep. Joy had read that the steepest recommended green roof was a 7:12 pitch (30°), so she made sure she hit that value.

A standard EPDM roof liner was used as the surface membrane, and several applications of liquid flashing with fibreglass cloth reinforcing was used on all the edges. Spray-applied open cellular insulation was applied to the underside of the structure to allow a full 12.5 cm (5 in) depth for growing medium.

The original concept for slope control was an expanded cellular geofabric typically used for road bed reinforcing. It is permeable and lightweight, yet extremely rigid when the fabric cells are expanded. It is also very expensive, however, so Joy looked for different solutions.

Installation

Because the concept of a green roof was very new to western New York, there were no skilled contractors in the area to install the roof. Joy was fortunate, however, to have also designed the green roof for a local university, and that was being constructed at the same time.

Lichtenfels Nursery from Johnstown, Pennsylvania, were installing the roof design at Niagara University and agreed to come out and review the project site. Joy's firm is very committed to sharing knowledge and promoting collaborative efforts in the profession. After a lengthy discussion with Lichtenfels, they decided to host an event that would promote the use of green roofs but also provide an opportunity to hear directly from the architect, the landscape architect, and the installer about how the roof worked. The result was a live installation demonstration and continuing education credit event for architects, landscape architects, and engineers. More than sixty professionals, educators, and students attended the event, which won a communications award from the New York Upstate Chapter of the American Society of Landscape Architects.

Because the original slope stabilization material was abandoned due to cost considerations, the team needed to rethink this crucial element. In the end the entire roof assembly went together very much like a quilt, and it started with the slope stabilization. The first layer was the typical moisture retention blanket with shovel guard. Zip ties were then heat welded to the fabric at about 5-cm (2-in) intervals. An interlocking slope stabilization panel was used as the primary slope mitigation, but its attachment to the roof needed to be retrofitted to the roof shell. Stainless steel eye bolts were used at 30-cm (12-in) intervals along the ridge line of the roof and then the slope panels were stitched with stainless steel cable to the eye bolts. Essentially the panel hangs from the ridge line and the zip ties are pulled through the panel.

Growing medium was then placed into the panel. A geofabric grid was placed on top of the growing medium, and the zip tie continued to be pulled through like a stitch in a quilt. A second layer of growing medium was placed on top of the geofabric. A final erosion control layer of burlap was placed on top of that, and the zip ties were pulled tight.

In an effort to be as efficient and sustainable as possible, Joy used the same materials and growing medium as in the Niagara University installation. She was able to work with the installers to use materials they already had in stock for this small roof installation, and was open to using plant materials the installer already had as well. Joy says, 'The only plant I really wanted was a native strawberry vine and we could not locate it at the time of the installation.'

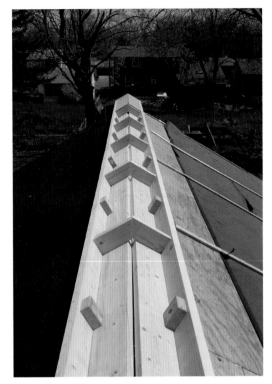

Top left: The roof was installed as a live performance and continuing education event for local practitioners. Photo by JKLA Studio

Above: The ridge detail. Photo by JKLA Studio

Center left: Placing the waterproof membrane. Photo by JKLA Studio

Left: The geofabric grid over the substrate. Photo by JKLA Studio

Plug plants were spaced throughout the roof and slices were made into the burlap cover to place the plant within the assembly. The roof has four sedums ranging in colour from yellow, white, pink, to red; several reed grasses (*Calamagrostis*); Russian sage (*Perovskia atriplicifolia*); and a perennial geranium. In the autumn of 2009, yarrow (*Achillea*) and the native strawberry vine (*Vitis*) they originally intended were added, as well as 500 grape hyacinth (*Muscari*) bulbs.

Success of the green roof

The roof has performed extremely well. There has not been any erosion on the slope, and the plants have shown marked growth over the past three growing seasons. Some weeds have infiltrated the roof, but nothing extensive as of yet. A Norway maple is located adjacent to the roof, and some saplings have taken root, but they do not reach any significant size. Dandelions have started to infiltrate, and these and the saplings have been removed during maintenance. Joy elected to leave a few of the native grasses that infiltrated, such as goldenrod (*Solidago*). 'It is difficult to keep this grass out of the roof, so we decided to embrace it rather than fight it,' says Joy.

The roof is very animated with wildlife as well. Birds, butterflies, and bees are present continuously from spring through autumn. The *Muscari* bulbs were a bit of an experiment, considering how the squirrels might react. It was a successful installation that did not result in squirrel damage. The grasses were trimmed back for the first winter, but Joy notes, 'This past year we left the grasses high to get the full winter effect, and it was stunning.' Trimming them in the spring did mean some bulb damage, but earlier spring trimming will help to avoid this in the future.

'The best benefit for me personally is that I get to see it every day from the window in my hallway. I see it in every season, every weather condition, and it is simply amazing,' says Joy. She, her colleagues, and family have enjoyed studying it, noting which plants are doing well and which are not performing as well. They have tested the stormwater runoff in real time by emptying the rain barrels on each side and then measuring after a rain event. During a two-hour

The best benefit for me personally is that I get to see it every day from the window in my hallway. I see it in every season, every weather condition, and it is simply amazing.

storm in July, the green roof side had about 15 cm (6 in) and the asphalt side filled the 230-L (50-gallon) barrel. Joy posts the photos and measurements on the company's blog and Facebook page for real-time reporting. They have also used the roof for educational events for community college horticulture programmes to the local third graders, highlighting the need for stormwater management and how green roofs mitigate runoff in the urban infrastructure.

'Everyone who sees the roof loves it,' says Joy. 'We have had random people stop by and ask to see the roof, including an elderly woman from Niagara Falls who drove around until she found us and a local high school science teacher. The usual reaction is awe and then the persistent question of "How do we cut the grass?"' The roof is a great conversation starter, and clients are always asking about it.

Joy also had her son's third grade class out for a visit. They showed the class photos from the construction and the plants on the roof, and then walked them through a demonstration of runoff using slate tiles and sponges. The next day, Joy's company received a booklet from the class summarizing their visit. The children really got it and could articulate how a green roof works.

NIGEL'S NOTES

Joy's roof demonstrates a successful technique for greening a steeply sloping roof. The idea of a live installation and performance, with an ongoing commentary, as a training programme has a lot of potential.

WHEELER STREET LEANGREEN HOUSE

Berkeley, California, United States • Owner and designer: **Jennifer Natali and Brian Kallay** • Context: **Residential** • Size: **12 m² (130 sq ft)** • Main purpose of green roof: **Rooftop food production, stormwater management, create new growing space in small yard, experiment, demonstration**

JENNIFER AND Brian have a small residential lot, and their backyard is 60 m² (625 sq ft) in area. Their new backyard shed (3 × 3.6 m, 10 × 12 ft) was built as a wood workshop and tool stores while Jennifer and Brian renovated their house. They wanted to replace the lost gardening space taken up by the new shed, and they also wanted to experiment with methods for managing stormwater on site. As a student in landscape architecture at University of California, Berkeley, Jennifer had learned about green roofs from a course in landscapes for Mediterranean climates (which describes much of California), focusing on stormwater. When she had the opportunity, she wanted to make one of her own.

Designing and planning

Jennifer and Brian planned and designed the roof themselves using drawings, models, and mock-ups. The process was a design-build sequence of different phases, somewhat stop-and-go, and not all planned at once prior to building. It was the first stand-alone structure they ever built, and they took an experimental approach. In general, they designed and built the shed structure, then designed and built the roof structure, drainage, and waterproofing. For the past two years, Jennifer and Brian have been playing with the vegetation. In between each phase, they spent a lot of time researching and sourcing materials. They had strict requirements about material reuse, life cycle, ease of installation, and cost.

Jennifer and Brian also visited two other small green roofs, both of which had used an EPDM waterproofing layer. One was a sedum-and-grass roof at a community garden shed (straw-bale construction) where she did a measured drawing of the rafters and cross section. They also volunteered to help restore a five-year-old roof at the Ecohouse in Berkeley, where the soil had become depleted of nutrients and the plants had mostly died. Jennifer and Brian helped remove vegetation and old soil, mix new soil, and bucket it up to the roof. The process allowed them to see how it all worked.

Installation

It was completely DIY. They aimed to use very accessible, low-tech materials and methods. Jennifer says, 'We didn't want to buy someone else's proprietary,

The first trays were placed on drainage material, and later trays went directly onto the roof. Photo by Jennifer Natali

plastic-intensive design. We didn't know anyone who had built a green roof at this small scale, we couldn't afford to pay them, and we were eager to learn since we were about to embark on renovating our whole house.'

They first planned the structure of the shed to handle the load of soil on the roof. That led them to a timber-frame structure using salvaged Douglas fir timbers with mortise and tenon joints (no screws or bolts). They modelled it with balsa wood at first, and then we practiced making mortise and tenon joints with scrap wood.

Throughout, Jennifer and Brian tried to use as much salvaged and reused material as possible. All the timbers, rafters, and finish surfaces were salvaged, sourced from reuse centres and salvage yards. They did buy new 20-mm (0.75-in) tongue-and-groove plywood for the roof deck. Because they installed a 150-mm (6-in) high tray (or rake) around the perimeter of the roof deck using salvaged bleachers (seating benches from tiered spectator stands at sports fields) from a local high school (complete with chewed gum and graffiti!), they needed to drill drain holes in this edge and build up a cricket— a ridge that would divert water to exit through the holes. 'That was more challenging than expected and involved rolling rubber balls down the roof to test how a drop of water would drain,' says Jennifer. They designed a two-drain system. They have been harvesting the rainwater in buckets and reusing it to irrigate the roof, but then needed larger storage containers.

For waterproofing, they first considered using EPDM due to its durability and longevity and lots of documented use in green roof construction. But Jennifer and Brian have been avoiding materials that require intensive processing (in terms of energy), petroleum in their manufacturing, or toxic by-products, as well as products that are shipped long distances or need to be replaced. EPDM would have to be shipped from far away, and they would be wasting part of the sheet in cutting it to fit the roof. They were using the shed roof as a test run for a larger 35 m² (380 sq ft) house roof. For Jennifer and Brian, large EPDM sheets seemed unwieldy and too expensive to ship.

Using a regional green building resource website, they found a locally produced acrylic elastomeric waterproofing product called Metacrylics. It's a DIY-friendly cold-mixed coating. Jennifer says, 'We drove to pick it up right where it's manufactured, and we were able to talk to the people who made it.' The application process was very accessible: it only required a paint roller, scissors, and gloves. Metacrylics has low levels of volatile organic compounds, so they were not concerned about inhaling fumes. It also contains recycled glass and fillers, and the manufacturer recycles and reuses the containers. Its durability seemed comparable to that of EPDM, especially in a green roof situation where it has no ultraviolet exposure. The worst case scenario seemed like a maintenance recoat in ten years rather than ripping off a membrane. According to the manufacturer, the runoff, although not certified as potable, is clean (given a first flush rinse). Unlike other white elastomerics, Metacrylics does not contain zinc, so it doesn't chalk and pollute the runoff. Jennifer says, 'I am tempted to have runoff from the roof tested since we are using it to irrigate our vegetables and could possibly use the stored rainwater for drinking if we have an earthquake disaster.'

Once the roof was waterproofed, Jennifer and Brian's approach to planting was also experimental. The roof surface immediately provided a place for them to start their vegetable seedlings for the garden. They already had some standard 425-mm (17-in) square planting trays made from black plastic with 75-mm (3-in) high walls and a plastic mesh base. They lined the base of the trays with landscaping fabric and filled it with coconut coir. 'I germinated most seeds indoors in paper towels and then planted one vegetable per tray,' says Jennifer. At first they placed the trays on leftover Miradrain, the dimpled plastic sheets used to help drain water away from building foundations. Jennifer used a drainage layer because she thought it was an absolute requirement based on

Above: The underlying structure of the roof. Photo by Jennifer Natali

Top right: The drainage chevron or 'cricket' that diverts water to the drainage holes on the sloping roof. Photo by Jennifer Natali

right: Applying the liquid waterproofing with a roller. Photo by Jennifer Natali

her research about green roofs. Water drained well because they built the roof plane on a 1:12 slope (5°). 'I cannot recall how we came up with this slope, but it was probably more of an aesthetic choice (based on our design drawings) than about drainage. It also matches the roof slope of our house.' The next row of trays did not use the Miradrain, and it also drained just fine. Based on checks after a rainfall, water did not pond and was retained within the soil.

Being able to start seeds on the roof has greatly expanded our garden space by allowing us to orchestrate a rotation of vegetables throughout our long growing season.

The coconut coir dried out quickly, requiring more frequent watering—twice a day by hand with a watering can filled with reused rainwater or captured roof irrigation water or, as the dry summer wore on, with the garden hose from the outside tap. Some plants responded to the dry-out by going to seed or yellowing. Jennifer remembers, 'I was upset that I was using so much water. What good is saving stormwater if I'm using up all the water that's piped halfway across California from a far-away river to our tap?' So they experimented with the soil mix and now use three-eighths coconut coir, three-eighths household compost, one-eighth composted

grape seeds, one-eighth chicken manure, and a dash of crushed lava rock and sometimes Douglas fir fines (0.25 in or less) for lightening the weight and diversifying the texture. The lava rocks were obtained free—shovelled from someone's 1970s-era residential landscaping and then crushed with a tamper on their sidewalk. Jennifer says, 'I now usually water every other day, but sometimes more, if it's over 80 degrees [27°C] or there's a dry wind, which is rare.'

Success of the green roof

The soil mix is lightweight and the shed is structurally solid. Besides the timbers, it was inexpensive to build. For the tray system, Jennifer estimates a cost of $2.20 per square foot. Bees have been visiting the roof, and native plants have begun to spring up.

The roof has turned out to have many benefits for food growing. 'Being able to start seeds on the roof has greatly expanded our garden space by allowing us to orchestrate a rotation of vegetables throughout our long growing season,' says Jen. Tender vegetable seedlings do better on the roof than in the ground, where they get attacked by slugs or trampled by the neighbourhood cats. The roof sits above it all and has much more access to sunlight than the garden, which gets shaded at one time or another by all the fences, buildings, and trees, and they are able to reuse any water that runs off for irrigating the vegetables once the rain stops. 'My dad said, "Jen, you are so practical." I don't think he ever would've imagined someone could (or would) grow vegetables on a roof . . . and he's a farmer!'

'We love the view from the roof. You can see over the fences to all the greenery of the neighbours'

Vegetables are started as seedlings on the roof, then planted out in the garden beds in a constant cycle. Strawberries are grown permanently on the rooftop and are free from slugs. Photo by Jennifer Natali

backyards, listen to the hummingbirds, and lay down to catch some sunshine when the house is still cold. Our neighbours can see what we're doing and it generates conversation, especially with the kids next door,' say Jennifer. They also have a view of the plants on the shed roof from the house. The 2.7-m (9-ft) height on the low slope of the roof is great for moving plants, soil, and water up and down. They use a movable ladder, allowing room for a compost pile and worm bin in this working area of the garden.

I am tempted to have runoff from the roof tested since we are using it to irrigate our vegetables and could possibly use the stored rainwater for drinking if we have an earthquake disaster.

But there are also problems with the food-growing roof. The plants depend on the very regular visits for water, especially in California's dry summer. Jen notes, 'It's not easy for a house-sitter to water if we ever go on vacation.' The vegetable seedlings require transplanting to allow for better spacing as they grow. This is time intensive, about one day per month. Some plants (especially broccoli) don't like the shallow trays and either get stunted (irrecoverable even if planted in the garden) or start flowering. Jennifer and Brian are still learning the culture and requirements of each vegetable seedling and best times and methods for transplant, so they are not using the space optimally just yet and they've had a few crop failures.

The roof gives them a view into the neighbours' yard, which makes Jennifer and Brian feel like they're invading their privacy every time the roof is watered. When watering with a hose (as opposed to a can), there's much more wasted water running off the walkway surface. But using a can is time intensive. If they had a tap on the roof, that would save trips up and down the ladder to fill each can of water. To reuse more water, they need larger rainwater harvesting containers which are expensive and/or ugly.

Jen says, 'I wish I could find deeper, nonplastic trays for the seedlings. I wish I could heat up the roof in the winter to extend the growing season. I wish I could grow coconut coir (or the equivalent) in our yard. But it's not a static setup, so I'm glad we can continue to experiment, and we hope to expand operations to the bigger house roof next year. Given the height differences, we may move the perennial strawberries to the higher roof (with irrigation) and fill the shed roof with veggie trays.'

Overall, Jen and Brian are happy with their green roof. They are able to grow more food on their small lot, to recycle more water, and to reduce the lot's stormwater impact. The roof provides a restorative new space to hang out in the garden—a benefit they didn't foresee at the start—and more interesting conversations with their neighbours. Also, they pay more attention to the birds and bees buzzing above the yard. Jen says, 'All in all, we are happy that all our research and design mock-ups were so successful. The roof hasn't fallen in yet! Playing pinball as we tested the cricket and drainage holes was a lot of fun.'

NIGEL'S NOTES

This is such an inspiring project. Jen and Brian researched all aspects meticulously, but have not been afraid to experiment and try out new ideas. They also show that it is worth persevering with trial and error, and that a green roof can be cost-effective if inexpensive and reclaimed materials are used in new ways. There is so much interest in food growing on rooftops, but very little experience of doing it for real. Jen shows us that we don't have to try and do everything on a rooftop, but that the roof can be an excellent protected starting point for young plants. It is also worth noting that the growing medium on this roof is rich in organic matter to retain as much water as possible for the plants.

RUDLIN GARDEN SHED

The completed shed. Photo by Helene Rudlin

Whalley Range, Manchester, United Kingdom • Owner and designer: **Helene and David Rudlin** • Context: **Garden shed** • Size: **2.5 × 3.5 m (8 × 11.5 ft)** • Main purpose of green roof: **Horticulture, aesthetic, biodiversity**

WHEN HELENE purchased her house thirteen years ago, she had no garden at the back, but an old traditional garage with two large doors with a pitch roof covered with flat red tiles. She decided to remove the garage and to construct a veranda using one of the garage walls which had three little panelled windows. She also kept the structure of the garage's back wall along with the beams and built a den for her children, with a ladder and a climbing rope. She then created a small garden with a large raised bed made of railway sleepers which now has all the family's fruiting bushes. Once the children abandoned the den and became teenagers, Helene decided to build a large shed with a green roof. She ran a gutter between the shed's roof and the veranda to collect rainwater from the veranda and the green roof.

Biodiversity was one of the main reasons for creating the green roof, as opposed to noise reduction, but also it was to give Helene an extra space to plant herbs and perennials and be a den and refuge for her cats and herself. Aesthetically, it is also very pleasing from the house's first floor windows, and the neighbours on both sides very much enjoy looking out onto another level of the garden. They like to see the drifts of grasses and flowers across the sky from their garden, and it has become a busy shortcut for the family's prowling cats. Birds, bees, and insects have settled there, too.

Helene helped with the creation of a green roof in Reddish Vale Community Garden and attended the World Green Roof Conference in London in 2008. She became very interested with the possibilities of creating more green spaces in cities and neighbourhoods. At the time she was thinking of changing career and was studying horticulture and garden design. Helene says, 'Also I am very much still a kid at heart, and the idea of climbing onto a roof and finding myself in a secret place, covered of wildflowers and herbs, is also very appealing. . . . I am a French national, and I have lived in many flats in many major cities in France and England. Balconies have always attracted me. The chance to have a little green space to myself high above the streets and grow what I can is the first thing I looked for when I moved into a flat.'

Designing and planning

Helene's husband David is a DIY wizard in his spare time, as well as a town planner. She is a gardener by profession and about to finish a garden design diploma. She is also a permaculture practitioner. They are both very fond of wood and have built everything from their beds to the green roof. Helene and David had an idea for sometime about how they could use the space to its full potential. Once they designed the shed, the roof became obvious. Helene says, 'Nature will always find itself a nook or a cranny to settle in and grow, regardless how well designed is the roof. I am interested in herbs and wildflowers and do not consider any plant a weed as such. The seeds are food for the birds and the leaves a habitat for the bugs. I wanted it to look natural and be useful in terms of a food source for our family.' In the roof's second year, ragged robins (*Lychnis flos-cuculi*), wild mallows (*Malva*), and orange hawkweeds (*Hieracium aurantiacum*) had found their way onto the roof.

Installation

Helene says, 'The satisfaction of doing it all ourselves was really rewarding. We are also very fussy and know exactly what we want. It was quite an undertaking, especially hoisting all the bags of gravel and soil onto the rooftop. But it was also a lot of fun, and we are blessed with two strong sons who helped and gained a beautiful suntan in the process.'

They used a variety of reclaimed and recycled wood, including old floor boards from their kitchen for joists. Two of the old garage's beams were placed across the length to support the joists on top. Then they placed the plywood and laid a tarpaulin, then a 10-cm (4-in) layer of gravel, and then a mix of topsoil from the front garden and homemade compost to a depth of about 15 cm (6 in). The roof is tilted slightly towards the veranda so that the water would drain into the gutters. They edged the roof with scaffolding planks and made four holes at each corner at the base to let as much water drain as possible. Helene says, 'I had experienced using a mix of LECA and soil—but I wanted to make the green roof as cheaply and green as possible.' All the roof materials are recycled, given, or found, with the exception of the tarp and the Forest Stewardship Council–certified marine plywood from their local timber merchant. Helene was worried about the plywood but was told it was made with environmentally friendly wood and not teak.

Success of the green roof

The green roof is in its fourth year now and is looking splendid. Helene and David were given an unknown grass as a gift from a friend which turned out to be a pampas grass (*Cortaderia*). It grew far too big and had to be pulled out. Helene says, 'The only problem I have found is that the depth isn't, well, that deep, and consequently the roots of all the plants have created a tangled, thick mat. I find it difficult to introduce a plant in there now.' The roof has lots of ox-eye daisies (*Leucanthemum*) which self-seeded mainly at the centre. These have to be divided so that the chamomile and marjoram don't have to fight for ground too much. There's the odd dandelion here and there, which the bees seem to like, and

The roof on the shed being planted. Photo by Helene Rudlin

a few geums and potentillas peak through the red fox sedge (*Carex buchananii*) and foxtail grass clumps. One lavender of two survived, but it seems to struggle a bit. Helene wishes the roof could have had at least 30 cm (12 in) of soil to provide enough growing space for vegetables. She says, 'I tried peas, the variety 'Feltham First', but they cascaded over the edge of the roof and dried out too quickly.'

Helene and David are really happy with the final green roof. It isn't quite like they imagined it would be—it is even better. The vegetation on the roof is really wild. Helene says, 'We can admire it from our dining room as if it was a small hanging garden of Babylon.' They have since created another eight rectangular windows in the veranda and lifted its roof so that they can see the whole green roof throughout the year. Helene likes to go up there in the sunshine and read or drink coffee. 'It smells beautiful sitting in the chamomile and marjoram, and I only wish I had more room to create another bigger one!'

Helene says, 'Anyone seeing the green roof for the first time goes "Wow!"' Often people don't really understand how or why the vegetation is up there, but they eventually realize that it is on the shed. The green roof is peculiar because of the maturity and the choice of plants. People don't expect a fully grown pampas or the other clumps of grasses, the marguerites swaying in the wind, and the chamomile cascading over the edge. Helene and David have interested many friends in building their own green roofs and convinced them that they do not require vast sums of money or professional building skills. If the structure is solid, anything can be grown up there.

'Two years ago a friend entered me in the Manchester in Bloom competition, which I reluctantly accepted,' says Helene. 'I wasn't sure my garden would be what they'd be looking for. . . . I thought my backyard and its green roof would be too quirky as I used lots of found items as containers and even my old bike is a raspberry climbing frame.' The garden won second prize in the Best Environmentally Friendly Garden category and the following year a second prize for Best Biodiversity Garden. 'I am overwhelmed how much we have moved on in terms of garden designs and the environmental ethos many of us now follow. Just taking part and seeing many other gardeners and gardens during the event has been brilliant.'

If Helene and David could do another roof, they would build it deeper. Although they see sedum green roofs as beautiful in their own right, they are more interested in growing food plants.

NIGEL'S NOTES

This project shows how a green roof can be the only garden area where space is limited. Helene has really made the very best of the opportunity she had, for a multilevel back yard to create a special personal refuge. Her idiosyncratic plant choices and the exuberant effect she has achieved show that there is no need to be bound by the orthodox views of what is and isn't achievable.

ANCAYA GARDEN SHED

Raleigh, North Carolina, United States • Owner and designer: **Emilio and Kathryn Ancaya of Living Roofs, Inc.** • Context: **Private residential, garden building** • Size: **2.5 × 3.0 m (8 × 10 ft)** • Main purpose of green roof: **Reduce stormwater runoff, provide habitat for birds and pollinating insects, aesthetic**

THIS NEW shed was part of the redesigned backyard landscape which included a fruit and vegetable garden, workshop, greenhouse, and green-roofed garden shed. Emilio and Kathryn Ancaya were in the process of redesigning their backyard and needed a garden shed, and they decided this would be a perfect place for a trial green roof. They knew the garden shed roof would be very visible from the house, so they wanted to integrate the building as best they could into the landscape. Additionally, they wanted to attract birds and pollinators to the roof.

Designing and planning

Although they now own a green roof company, Emilio and Kathryn built the shed as their first green roof project, long before the company was formed. The experience was key to their discovery of the potential of green roofs. Emilio and Kathryn designed the structure themselves, based on information from Ed Snodgrass at Emory Knoll Farms, the internet, and various books. 'The most challenging part was designing the drains. We came up with our own solution which works great,' says Emilio.

Installation

A standard waterproofing membrane was fixed to the roof. On top of this was placed a root barrier, a permeable landscape weed block fabric. Because the roof has a 7:12 (30°) slope, a wood grid system was used to keep the substrate on the roof. The grid was elevated 20 mm (0.75 in) above the roof surface to enable water to drain beneath. Substrate was laid to a depth of 10 cm (4 in) and was composed of a 4:1 mix of expanded shale and compost. Vegetation was introduced as plug or pot-grown plants grown by Emilio or obtained from Emory Knoll Farms and included species of *Delosperma, Sedum, Talinum, Euphorbia*, and *Sempervivum*. The roof is watered very occasionally using a garden hose, and an annual application of organic slow-release fertilizer is applied.

Success of the green roof

The roof has delivered many benefits and has been a great success. According to Emilio, the only

The completed shed. Photo by Emilio Ancaya, Living Roofs, Inc.

challenge is the roof ridge, which dries faster than the rest of the roof. 'The view of the shed from anywhere in the backyard is definitely a great sight to see,' says Emilio. The green roof significantly reduces stormwater runoff as compared to a traditional roof (such as asphalt shingles, metal) and the roof definitely attracts birds and pollinating insects. Every spring small sunflowers sprout on the roof. These seeds are dropped by birds who feed on the roof after

Cooling was not expected but is a great additional benefit: the building is a cool retreat during hot summer temperatures.

Talinum calycinum flowering freely. Although short-lived, this species readily seeds from year to year. Photo by Emilio Ancaya, Living Roofs, Inc.

visiting the bird feeders. Cooling was not expected but is a great additional benefit: the building is a cool retreat during hot summer temperatures. And the roof has been a great learning experience, as it was the first of many green roofs for Emilio and Kathryn.

If starting again with the roof, Emilio says that he would do some things differently. They would add water retention fabric under the entire system to help retain or at least slow water drainage, as well as an additional layer over the ridge to help retain moisture along the dry peak. Finally, they would have cut the rafter tails back further from the roof deck edge, because water comes in contact with the rafter tails for prolonged periods when the roof drains.

The green roof after seven years. Water drains from the roof into the pond. Photo by Andy Clayden

Andy used lead flashing to cover the liner at the edges, giving a crisp edge detail.

The growing medium was a mixture of LECA (expanded clay), soil, and peat. Andy filled the edges of the roof with pea gravel to aid drainage and wrapped this in a geotextile. Drainage off the roof was through a hole cut in the plywood and an inserted tank connector (plumbing fixing), sealed with silicon. A piece of geotextile membrane was placed over the hole to prevent clogging. Rain chains were used to divert water from the roof to ground level, where a channel cut through the veranda deck allows water to run into the pond.

The roof was originally planted with sedums

Right: The original planting used sedums, with a turf edge, divided by a wooden framework. Photo by Nigel Dunnett

Below: The building in winter with dead stems poking through the snow. Photo by Andy Clayden

> *Relax a bit, and don't give in to the urge to be too tidy. It can look fantastic in winter with long bright dead stems.*

ordered from a specialist supplier, and the edge was turfed to prevent erosion while the plants established. 'I had tried using a textile over the roof to prevent erosion, but I found this difficult to work with, so I took it off,' says Andy. He also placed a timber grid over the roof using roofing laths, which helped to contain the soil and provided a framework for the planting. The grid created a mosaic pattern, but is now invisible now that the roof vegetation has matured.

Success of the green roof

'The roof was a real conversation piece from the start,' says Andy. The sedums generally have been less successful, and the more ornamental cultivars have not succeeded. The roof is now a much more diverse mix of grasses, thrift, alliums, and even some self-seeded *Miscanthus* grass. Andy now leaves it alone apart from occasional trimming. When the roof was first getting established he did add water, but this may have made it too wet for the sedums. The roof has even had reeds and strawberries growing along the gutter edge. Fat hen (*Chenopodium album*) was a problem weed at first but has died out.

In the future, Andy would not plant sedums. 'They are just too dull, and there are many more interesting things that can go on a small domestic roof. Give yourself some depth of growing medium, and be prepared to garden your roof and find out what works for you. Relax a bit, and don't give in to the urge to be too tidy. It can look fantastic in winter with long bright dead stems.' In addition, he would replace the LECA with a reclaimed crushed aggregate and use a peat-free alternative.

NIGEL'S NOTES

Andy's roof was an early example of putting a small extensive roof onto a garden building in the United Kingdom, when the general impression at the time was that a pristine, sedum-only carpet was the only solution. Andy's experience shows that, unless one is prepared to constantly weed out invaders, it is far better to accept that green roofs are dynamic and will change according to conditions. Andy's roof is now much more diverse and virtually self-sustaining. The project also demonstrates a really effective approach to capturing and using all the rainwater runoff from the building.

Langdon Hills, Essex, United Kingdom • Owner: **The Hurter family** • Green roof consultant: **John Little** • Context: **Private garden building** • Size: **3.6 × 4 m (12 × 13 ft)** • Main purpose of green roof: **Recreation**

LIZ AND Mike Hurter have a house and garden perched on top of the west side of Langdon Hills in Essex, southeast England. They have a large garden and love the potential for buildings, plants, and socializing it offers. Liz and Mike had promised their two teenage children a 'bolt hole,' somewhere of their own to escape to, and so the idea of a new building in the garden was born. They also hoped to somehow combine this new youth den with space of their own to use as a home office (a compromise they later regretted).

The house and garden are sited on one of the few hills in this part of Essex, and the Hurters were keen to maximize the view. They look out across the flat Essex countryside and can see the tower blocks of Canary Wharf in the distance, poking through the London haze. The view from the new roof would be uninterrupted by the hedges and trees at garden level, but, being on higher ground, the site is very exposed.

Their children attended the local primary school, where three green roofs had already been built on storage sheds and veranda roofs. Liz soon discovered that they had been constructed by a local company, the Grass Roof Company. John Little, one of the partners in the company, also had children at the school. After a few informal chats with John in the school yard, Liz was convinced she wanted to green her new roof. The Hurters wanted a roof that would be easy to maintain and could function as an open space for sunbathing. Liz thought a flat grass roof would do all this and give her the living roof that she had become convinced was right for her.

Designing and planning

The roof sits atop a timber building designed under the strict guidance of their children, Emily and James. It uses Forest Stewardship Council–certified timber and logs from the local country park. Fully glazed doors front and rear ensure good light levels and access to the large garden that surrounds the structure. As the building began to take shape, it soon became clear to Liz and Mike that the kids were keen to restrict access to the roof to themselves and their friends. After some persuasion, the design incorporated a drawbridge so that a section of the steps to the roof could be lifted, once the kids were up there. Liz hoped the building would blend into the surroundings, and wanted 'a cute-looking shed.'

The completed building, with external access and drawbridge to roof level. Photo by John Little

She had originally thought about a long grass ramp to gain access to the roof, although practical considerations made this impossible.

Installation

The roof has 200 × 50 mm (8 × 2 in) joists set at 400 mm (16 in) apart. This close spacing was used so that the roof could cope with the extra weight of a kids' party. The roof deck is 18-mm (0.7-in) ply, and the 1-mm (0.04-in) butyl rubber waterproofing was sandwiched between two layers of geotextile. The upper layer of geotextile had to be particularly tough as the roof was going to take lots of wear. Instead of a conventional drainage mat, a gravel edge runs around the whole roof, taking excess water into the one 75-mm (3-in) outlet and down galvanized chains. A 100-mm (4-in) layer of soil from the building footings covers the roof, and drought-tolerant turf was

The thin screen to the building contains log sections in wire mesh panels. Photo by Jane Sebire

laid to finish. The building cost around £5000 in 2004.

Success of the green roof

Since being built, the kids seem to ignore the inside of the building, preferring to hang out on the roof. Adult visitors love it and cannot resist its appeal for drinks on the terrace. Other uses include sunbathing, stargazing, firework spotting, and chatting. It's a great place to sit and watch the sun disappear over London and makes picking fruit from the adjacent plum tree a positive pleasure. Another unforeseen use for the green roof is jumping off! The Hurters did consider installing a handrail for safety but settled for verbal warnings instead. When Liz was asked what wildlife she has seen, she replied 'Several teenagers visit regularly.'

The steps and platform access make cutting the roof with a trimmer feasible, but Liz still regrets not sticking to her grass ramp idea. She says, 'Getting a petrol mower up there would make maintenance much easier and would have looked great.' The original turf planting tends to dry out above the gravel drainage channels, so Liz has added sedums and says she will add more flowers to decorate and soften the roof edge. Other maintenance includes watering and removing wind-blown thistles, not much fun with bare feet. The leaky-pipe irrigation installed has proved to be not very effective, with the water running straight to the outlet before soaking into the soil. 'We have had to resort to a conventional sprinkler, not that convenient for a roof!' The roof structure would probably have allowed for a greater depth of soil, say 150 mm (6 in), which would have provided the grass with extra water and less reliance on irrigation. At the time of building it was not certain how much the extra load from a roof full of kids would add, so only 100 mm (4 in) was installed. Liz feels she may have to feed the roof and will probably use a conventional lawn fertilizer.

The roof has delivered a cool space both above and below to sit and chill out. It's given the building a very sturdy platform to sight see from, and the roof is guaranteed to resist all that the exposed site can throw at it. It is, however, a compromise between kids' den and home office. Liz wishes she had stuck

Other uses include sunbathing, stargazing, firework spotting, and chatting.

to her original plans and allowed the building to have a cosier, less formal feel. The shed has a bigger profile from the house than she had hoped, but qualifies this by adding that it is invisible from above. 'You can't see it at all on Google Earth,' she says.

Does Liz have any advice for others thinking about a grass roof? 'Yes, it would be a good place to keep a rabbit.'

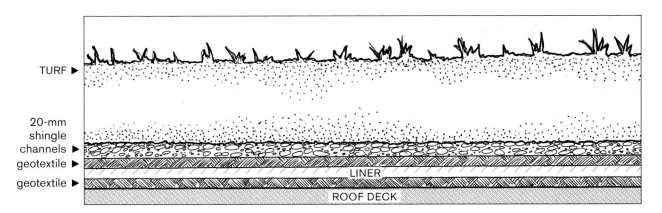

TURF ▶

20-mm shingle channels ▶
geotextile ▶
geotextile ▶

LINER

ROOF DECK

The green roof build-up. Drawing by Evangelia Bakratsa

JOYNER GARDEN SHED

Shenfield, Essex, United Kingdom • Owner: **Paul and Beverley Joyner** • Design: **John Little** • Context: **Private residential** • Size: **27 m² (290 sq ft)** • Main purpose of green roof: **Aesthetic, cooling**

THE JOYNER family live in Shenfield, Essex, a relatively affluent town with mostly medium to large houses and good-sized gardens. Paul works in finance, and Beverley runs a children's nursery. They have three children. In 1999 their house had a lot of improvement work, including a large double-storey extension that took away some of the garden and encouraged them to rethink their outdoor area. This loss of green space was one of the reasons Paul and Beverley thought of a living roof. The original shed Paul describes as an awful, typically dowdy structure tucked away in the top corner of the garden. From here the garden slopes down towards the house, and this was influential in the design of the replacement building. Behind the proposed site was a large hedge that provides shade for part of the day, and this shade proved to be important for the long-term development of the roof.

The 'posh shed,' as the new building came to be known, was needed to provide the family with a storage space for garden tools, a sleep-over area for the kids, and something different for the neighbours to contemplate. John Little, a partner in the local Grass Roof Company, had become friends with the Joyners and was keen to convince Paul and Bev how a new building with a living roof could deliver all of those things and with style.

Designing and planning

When they met to discuss the project, John enthusiastically explained the many benefits in terms of cooling the space, adding biodiversity, and increasing the life of the waterproofing. He soon realized that, from the few photos and information he had given them, Paul and Bev were already sold on the idea. The meeting concentrated on how the building could be designed to allow the family to see as much of the roof as possible from the house and the Joyner's preference for a sedum and herb planting design.

Installation

The Grass Roof Company were conscious that green roofs on smaller buildings can look top-heavy. To keep the roof in scale and the joist size to 150 mm (6 in), a centre beam was added to support the roof. Because the roof was to be open and visible from beneath, good-quality birch plywood was used; this also helped to add to the rigidity of the building,

The roof vegetation is very lush as a result of feeding and watering. Photo by John Little

an important consideration with the weight of a green roof. Despite Paul's 1.9 m (6 ft 3 in) frame, the Joyners were keen to bring the roof down as close to the eye line as possible. A veranda was added and head height compromised to try and bring the roof to the people, as it were.

In 2000 Erisco Bauder was one of the only suppliers and sources of advice for installing sedum blanket in the United Kingdom. Until then the Grass Roof Company had experience with basic soil and turf roofs, so relied on the information from the suppliers for the roof's composition. Although the quality and plant variety was excellent, on their advice the blanket was only laid on 30 mm (1.2 in) of mineral rockwool.

Success of the green roof

The building and roof were finished in April 2000, and the first year produced a flush of flowers from the sedums, chives, and dianthus in the pregrown mat. The pregrown blanket meant the roof had delivered a spectacular show in the first year. Paul and Bev were suitably impressed but were keen for the results to continue in subsequent years. Bev says that Paul's previous contact with green was from behind a rotary mower. He has now become a green roof evangelist, regularly quizzing John, 'Shall I water? Shall I take this plant out? What is the pink flower? Shall I fertilize?'

His enthusiasm did result in a carpet of purple fertilizer pellets (many times the correct rate), and this was combined with overwatering. While not the most sustainable approach, this again produced an amazing display, and for Paul the result is the green roof he loves. Paul says, 'The roof provides surprise and delight every day, it is always changing,' a comment that really shows why living roofs work on a human level. The roof has moved from the bright colours of the original plant mix to a more subtle alliance of sedums, grasses, chives, and wind-blown introductions that produce a more natural meadow feel to the roof. Paul is philosophical about the change and he accepts that it's not a manicured garden and. Because it's 'on the roof,' a more unkempt look is great—something that he and Bev would not necessarily accept at ground level. What would he change if he could start again? 'Not a thing.'

Paul feels the roof has given his family the working cabin that children can party in and a roof that can be seen clearly from the house and especially from the kids' bedrooms. He loves the way the roof is framed through the kitchen window as you walk through the house. The only maintenance over the last nine years, apart from the water and feeding, has been the addition of log piles and the removal of a few sow thistles, and for this he always sends the boys up. Easy!

The roof has moved from the bright colours of the original plant mix to a more subtle alliance of sedums, grasses, chives, and wind-blown introductions that produce a more natural meadow feel to the roof.

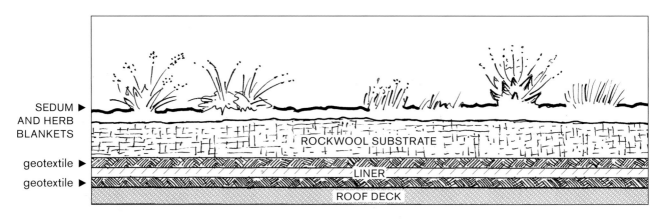

The green roof build-up. Drawing by Evangelia Bakratsa.

JOHN'S NOTES

I have now realized that relying on 30 mm (1.2 in) of mineral rockwool as a substrate for the roof does not deliver plant diversity in the long term. This substrate would normally mean the enduring vitality of the roof would be in question, but Paul's commitment to an annual feed and watering has meant the roof has continued to thrive. The combination of conditions that has shaped this roof is interesting. Shading for part of the day has helped to reduce the stress on the plants and allowed more species to survive. These factors, however, mean the roof is more prone to grass and weed species taking hold, where normally the heat of the summer would keep these to a minimum.

This is why the small-scale roof proves to be so diverse. It is individuals approaching a new potential green space with a mixture of very personal tastes and wishes, not a corporation driven just by an obligation to green itself. By their nature, small-scale roofs can be adapted and tailored in the same way as the gardens that often surround them.

CRUMMAY AND DHARMAPANI POTTING SHED

Birmingham, United Kingdom • Owner: **Tricia Crummay and Dharmapani** • Designer: **John Little** • Context: **Shed, garden building** • Size: **1.4 × 2.6 m (4.5 × 8.5 ft)** • Main purpose of green roof: **Aesthetic**

TRICIA CRUMMAY and Dharmapani's shed sits in the back garden of their house in Billesley, one of Birmingham's first council estates. Tricia, a photographer, and DP, a music teacher, both enjoy looking at alternative ways of doing things. So when they needed something as everyday as a potting shed, they looked for some way of moving it away from the norm. Their shed was to be in the bottom corner of the garden, overlooked by several adjacent houses. Her brother-in-law, John Little, offered to help with the building.

Designing and planning

They both love their outdoor space and so were keen not to lose any green when adding the shed to their garden. The green roof, they hoped, would help to cool the shed, look good, and with luck attract bees and butterflies—although as we see later some of the wildlife was more unusual.

Both DP and Tricia wanted the shed to keep as much of the original design and scale as possible.

They had seen green roof makeovers on television and did not want the external frame and heavy look of these early green roof adaptations. So John decided to strengthen the existing structure to handle the extra weight loading rather than tack on an external frame. Forest Stewardship Council–certified timber, organic paint, and recycled plastic were also preferred.

Installation

Extra timber uprights matching the existing ones were added to the walls and plywood sheets were fixed internally to strengthen and provide the rigidity a building with an extra 800 kg (1760 lb) on the roof would need. The potting shed had one wall of glass, so an extra support was fixed to act as a lintel over these windows and to ensure none of the weight from the new roof affected this side of the shed. In the same way, more roof joists were added to the few that supported the roof.

The building was now rigid and strong enough to support the living roof externally, although it looked the same as before. DP wanted the roof to work and last for the long term, so they decided not to rely on the felt waterproofing even though this was new. Instead they used a butyl rubber liner protected by tough geotextile above and below.

The completed shed. Photo by John Little

The existing roof was then adapted to suit. The shallow fascia was removed and a new deeper fascia was fixed, extending up above the roof edge, and this was then decorated with organic paint. To help spread some of the roof load, 12-mm (0.5-in) plywood was put on top of the felt and fixed down through the roof deck and into the joist work. A triangular timber known as an arris rail was then screwed to the ply and new fascia to tie these together. The water-proof liner was then laid over the edge of the roof and secured with a timber side cap to form a drip. Recycled plastic was then fixed to form a top cap and cover the exposed liner. A gap in the fascia on the lowest side of the roof allows the excess water to drain off.

Tricia had discussed the plant choices for a green roof with John. After considering the conventional alternatives of sedum mat, meadow, or biodiverse, she decided on one of her own, 'heavy and lush.' To get this effect, a good depth of substrate would have to go on. John worked out that the roof would need to support around 200 mm (8 in) of substrate with a loading of 300 kg/m² (60 lb/sq ft). To continue the sustainable theme, crushed ceramics mixed with 10 percent green waste compost was used as a growing medium. Tricia thought old sinks and toilets on a

Edge detail. Photo by Jane Sebire

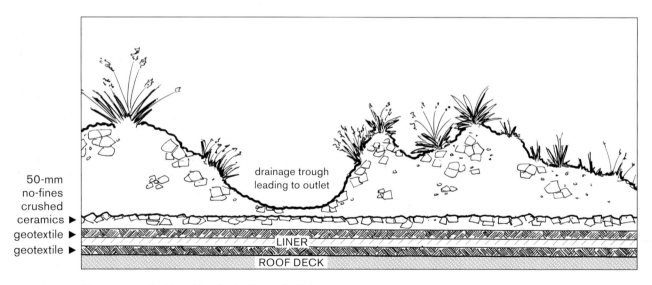

50-mm
no-fines
crushed
ceramics ▶
geotextile ▶
geotextile ▶

drainage trough
leading to outlet

LINER

ROOF DECK

The green roof build-up. Drawing by Evangelia Bakratsa

roof had a certain ring. The mix, although unproven, appealed to them both and John assured them 'something will grow.'

After this optimistic prediction, they all felt confident enough to go to the local nursery and buy some plants. They knew the roof would be a hostile and occasionally very dry place, so they opted for a range of sedums, succulents, and herbs, although the choice was limited as the garden centre was better known for its selection of ornaments and potting sheds than its range of plants. Tricia was given the job of planting the roof, only pausing long enough to pose for photos. As the budget for plants was limited, a green roof seed mix was oversown to supplement the planting.

Success of the green roof

At the time of writing, the roof has only just been planted. But already it has attracted lots of bees to the sedums. Indeed within a week they saw one of their neighbours using the vantage point to call for his lost parrot. Tricia and DP say the roof has given them a 'bonny shed' that delivers the feel-good benefits they wanted. Friends are intrigued, with one couple even choosing to include a turf roof in the plans for their new kitchen extension. Maintenance so far has simply meant watering the new planting. Tricia is relaxed about future work, 'We don't expect a garden on the roof, rather an unexpected green space that will have to change and adapt to the level of maintenance we are prepared to put in. None.'

JOHN'S NOTES

There is such potential in retrofitting small buildings. It was good to see how simple it is to strengthen the building without changing the original design. Converting a shed is a great way for people to get the confidence to green their house.

Tricia planting the roof. Photo by Jane Sebire

Kennett Square, Pennsylvania, United States • Owner and designer: **Margot Taylor Chalfant and Jefferson Chalfant** • Context: **Garden building, home retreat** • Size: **10 m² (108 sq ft)** • Main purpose of green roof: **Sustainable use of materials, aesthetic**

IN 1997 Margot visited the legendary Scottish garden and spiritual community Findhorn in Morayshire. During her four-month visit she fell in love, not just with Findhorn's way of life, but with the Nature Sanctuary, a small and magical building nestled into a large sand dune, built of earth, stone, and wood and topped with a grassy meadow.

When Margot returned to her Pennsylvania home, she brought with her the dream of creating a spiralling garden based on the Findhorn teachings, one anchored by a small hut that would emerge from the earth, hidden in a tapestry of vegetation, built of straw, and capped by a green roof. It would be a place intended for retreat and quiet contemplation, an ode to nature. What started as a garden feature quickly became a garden treasure.

In Margot's Pennsylvania township, structures under 11 m² (120 sq ft) do not require a building permit, which allowed for a more flexible and fluid design process. The project started with a building location, size parameters, and a loose budget.

Key to the project's success was finding the right contractor, someone with practical building experience and skill, a creative flare, a willingness to work small, and the courage to try something new. Eventually Margot found local builder Jeff Chalfant, who not only helped design and build the project, but, during the course of the project, also became her husband. When Jeff arrived for their first meeting with an intricately patterned, polished stone, asking Margot whether that was what she had in mind, Margot knew that she'd found her man.

Designing and planning

Margot guided the shape and style of the building, and Jeff brought fresh vision and brawn. Together, they agreed on a footprint inspired by a nautilus shell. Within the shell-like base, twenty-eight straw bales were stacked, wired, and sown tight, and sculpted by a saw for visual effect. Peach-hued plaster was applied on the inside, ochre-toned stucco on the outside. In time the interior space took form with glass-bottle light portals, cork floor, custom wood benches and door, fused glass windows, and tree-branch light sconces. For the outside, driftwood window sills, metallic tile embellishments, swirled stucco relief,

A chain carries runoff water from the roof into a reflecting pool below. Photo by Ed Snodgrass

and tooled copper rainspouts. One rainspout encircles a rusted chain that guides rainwater from the roof to a reflecting pool in front of the hut. The hut is heated in winter by a radiant floor, and cooled in summer by breezes. A tribute to patience, the entire process, building to roof, took four years.

Margot's decision for using green building methods was both environmental and aesthetic. Building green begins with using local resources. In Margot's community straw bales are readily available and

inexpensive. The choice of a vegetated roof was also easy with a wealth of local sources at hand for materials and design expertise. As at Findhorn, Margot wanted the roof form to flow with the site, and it does by arching in a gentle roll that simulates the surrounding landscape and serves for drainage.

Installation

Construction of the green roof was straightforward. Over the plywood roof form Jeff laid an EPDM liner,

The green roof design reflects the local landscape and blends the building with its surroundings. Photo by Ed Snodgrass

followed by a woven fibre layer and a plastic drainage sheet, all barriers to manage roots and water. A hose was run up through the hut wall and connected to a drip hose spread evenly on top, making it possible to irrigate the roof plants as needed. Rocks were positioned next to create deeper planting pockets and concentrate the material load onto principal structural members in the hut. Over this Jeff added 100–150 mm (4–6 in) of specially mixed, mostly inorganic green roof medium.

Locally procured plants were planted directly into the medium. Shallow-rooted and drought-tolerant perennials were selected as most capable of surviving the extreme climatic conditions of a roof environment. Plants included *Sedum aizoon* 'Euphorbioides', *Sedum sexangulare, Sedum album, Sedum spurium* 'Schorbusser Blut', *Sedum kamtschaticum, Sedum rupestre* 'Angelina', *Delosperma nubigenum, Dianthus arenarius,* and *Dianthus* 'Tiny Rubies'.

Success of the green roof

The random arrangement of plants and rocks on top mimics the natural patterns of rocks and water in streams characteristic of the region. Barely a year after completion, the green roof filled in. By the second year, the plantings evoked the qualities of local meadows with welcomed native perennials naturalizing within. The roof is now a distinctive extension of the garden.

The unconventional building materials selected for the hut are actually highly energy efficient. On the coldest days the hut is cosy while consuming minimal energy. Walls insulated by straw have a 44R value for efficiency, three times greater than other trade insulating materials. The green roof acts to insulate the hut by holding winter heat in and keeping excess summer heat out.

It is clear that green building strategies can lead to artful, creative, and whimsical solutions. What began as a garden folly emerged for Margot and Jeff, in their words, 'As a magical sanctuary in all seasons.'

Shallow-rooted and drought-tolerant perennials were selected as most capable of surviving the extreme climatic conditions of a roof environment.

Custer, Ohio, United States • Owner and designer: **Jane, Jack, and Hannah Phillips** • Context: **Garden shed** • Size: **2.5 × 3.0 m (8 × 10 ft)** • Main purpose of green roof: **Aesthetic**

JANE AND her builder husband, Jack, are modern pioneers, carrying out a twenty-first century version of a cherished tradition in America. They built their own log home, and they hunt for, slaughter, and process much of their meat. In addition to keeping a large perennial garden, they also grow and preserve as many of their own fruits and vegetables as they can.

Designing and planning

When Jane and Jack decided they needed a garden shed, she remembered pictures that her parents had taken on vacation in Alaska, showing green roofs on cabins there. 'When I saw them, I knew a green roof was for me,' Jane recalled. The shed roof was designed to blend with the landscape and fit with their log home. Jane read up on sheds and green roofs and decided to tackle the project largely by herself, with help from Jack and a new set of tools she'd received as a Christmas present.

Installation

The shed has a two-pitch, 2:12 (10°) roof, on which they first laid a decking of treated plywood, followed by EPDM pond lining material and a 5-cm (2 in) drainage layer of crushed stone, which was left over from their home's sidewalk construction. On top of that that they built a frame using 5 × 15 cm (2 × 6 in) boards with 5 × 10 cm (2 × 4 in) cross members that lay right on the stone. They deliberately left a little gap in the frame for the water to escape.

Capping the roof, Jane added 10 cm (4 in) of bagged organic soil for the plants. Beyond that, she gave little thought to what plants the roof would support. Jane merely divided some of her garden perennials and transplanted them to the roof.

Success of the green roof

Supplementing rainfall with daily watering, Jane kept the transplants alive and looking good. But when winter came, the plants all died. The 10 cm (4 in) of soil was simply not up to the task of sustaining many deep-rooted, water-loving plants. 'My big mistake was not researching what plants would work,' Jane acknowledges today.

Working with Emory Knoll Farms to develop a new plant list, Jane successfully replanted the entire roof with drought-hardy, shallow-rooted perennials,

The green roof looks good all year round. Here the sedums are in full flower. Photo by Jane Phillips

all of which have survived hot dry Midwestern summers without additional irrigation and several winters, as well. The plants include *Sedum album, Sedum spurium* 'Fuldaglut', *Sedum sexangulare, Sedum takesimense* 'Golden Carpet', *Delosperma nubigenum* 'Basutoland', and *Talinum calycinum*.

In addition, Jane notes that the roof has suffered very little erosion, just some settling. Despite the organic medium, the roof is not overrun with weeds. Jane estimates that she weeds her roof twice a year, deeming that sufficient.

The cost of installing the roof was minimal. Jane and Jack bought the treated plywood, pond-lining material, soil, and the new plants, which at $300

were the greatest expense they incurred. They used leftover scrap lumber for the frame and leftover crushed stone for the drainage layer.

Jane found the experience of installing a green roof so satisfying that she plans to install another one on a summer kitchen that she and Jack are planning. A large part of the appeal is how attractive she finds the roof throughout the year. 'Even in an ice storm the plants look beautiful,' she says. And Jane loves the attention it garners from visitors, all of whom are initially surprised and then very complimentary, she notes. 'Don't be afraid to build a green roof,' she advises everyone who asks. 'It's very rewarding and well worth it.'

Atlanta, Georgia, United States • Owner and designer: Bob Saul, Saul Nurseries • Context: **Demonstration roof** • Size: **2.5 × 2.5 m (8 × 8 ft)** • Main purpose of green roof: **Demonstrate plant and substrate use to nursery customers**

SAUL NURSERIES is one of the largest and most successful nursery businesses in the southeastern United States. Owned by two brothers, Richard and Bob Saul, the nursery is well known for its commitment to bringing new plants to market, some of them bred and patented in their state-of-the art tissue culture laboratory. Bob Saul designed the green roof to attract the attention of local landscape architects and installers who regularly purchase plants and soil at their wholesale location. The roof showcases a line of plants grown by the nursery specifically for green roofs, and the substrate used is one developed and marketed by the nursery. The Sauls hoped that the green roof would spark interest, not just for the concept of vegetated roofs, but specifically for the products used on it. The nursery also hoped to establish itself as an industry leader, showing its clients that it was on the cutting edge of a new trend in landscape design.

Designing and planning

Because the green roof was the centrepiece of the project, a display shed was newly constructed against an existing building to accommodate the roof. No formal plans were drawn up, however, and Saul used his own employees to construct the whole thing.

Installation

Beginning with two 100 × 100 mm (4 × 4 in) posts, they attached the frame to an existing building in a visible location on the nursery property. For the roof's decking the staff used marine plywood, acquired inexpensively at a local lumber yard. On top of that, they spread roofing tar as a sealant and then topped it with 6-mil polyethylene sheeting, all of which the nursery already had. Saul designed the extensive roof to be 2.5 × 2.5 m (8 × 8 ft), with a 1:8 (7°) slope, so that standing water would never be a problem, but also so that the green roof would not require a fully fledged drainage system.

The nursery used 100 mm (4 in) of its own trademarked green roof medium, ItSaul Natural, as the roof's substrate. ItSaul Natural consists of 80 percent mineral inorganic matter, 15 percent organic matter (worm castings), and 5 percent sand. Planted in the substrate is a mix of *Sedum* and *Delosperma*

The green roof is on a simple lean-to structure fixed to an
existing building. Photo by Ed Snodgrass

varieties, all of which Saul Nurseries grows and sells.
Plants include *Delosperma ashtonii, Delosperma cooperi, Delosperma nubigenum, Delosperma* 'Kelaides',
Sedum album 'Murale', *Sedum album* 'France', *Sedum
sexangulare, Sedum rupestre* 'Angelina', and *Sedum
kamtschaticum.*

Success of the green roof

The green roof was built in 2003 and is the second
oldest extensive green roof in Atlanta. Bob Saul is
very pleased with how it looks and has held up, and
he is especially satisfied with the nursery's green roof
medium. 'The only way you can tell if the soil is
good is with time, and this one looks very healthy,'
he says.

Asked whether he has had any problems with the
roof, Bob concedes that if he were to do it again, he
would probably use baffling to hold the medium
and plants in place, and he would use a more reliable root barrier. Also, because the green roof is on

a low shed—the front of the roof is at 1.5 m (5 ft), the rear at just over 1.8 m (6 ft)—the roof gets more tree seedlings than he anticipated and so requires weeding several times a year. Finally, the posts holding the roof up are beginning to warp, a fact that Bob attributes to the relatively inexpensive lumber used. Overall, the green roof cost was negligible, as mostly leftover materials were used and Bob incurred no additional labour costs beyond the time he was already paying his nursery employees.

The plants were irrigated on a regular basis until they were fully established, a practice Bob recommends for all green roofs for the first six months or so, depending on weather. 'It's such a small investment for keeping the roof alive,' he notes. Fertilizer, however, is not something that he recommends, and he used none on the nursery's green roof.

Bob notes that the green roof initially drew some sceptical comments and even laughter from its target audience. Now, he says, all the landscape architects are eager to learn more about it, noting that their customers are becoming interested in the concept. Because of the small size of the display green roof, Bob feels that it's very adaptable to residential applications, which is just what he had in mind to begin with. 'This is exactly what people will want their roof to look like.'

Bob concedes that if he were to do it again, he would probably use baffling to hold the medium and plants in place, and he would use a more reliable root barrier.

GREENSGROW FARMS

Philadelphia, Pennsylvania, United States • Owner and designer: **Mary Seton Corboy, cofounder of Greensgrow Farms** • Context: **City farm, education** • Size: **20 m² (215 sq ft)** • Main purpose of green roof: **Summer cooling**

The green-roofed building is a cold storage shed for vegetables grown on site. Photo by Nigel Dunnett

GREENSGROW FARMS is a city farm in North Philadelphia. It was created on the site of a former galvanized steel works in the late 1990s. The whole site is covered in concrete, and there is no natural soil. A wide range of heirloom vegetables and fruits are grown in large raised beds directly over the concrete—in effect they are like large green roofs on the ground—and lettuces are grown hydroponically. The farm sells directly to local restaurants, but also runs a community-supported agriculture scheme, whereby consumers buy a share in the farm and in return each week receive a box of vegetables and fruits produced on the farm.

The extensive, modular green roof at Greensgrow Farms sits on top of a refrigeration shed that is used for the storage of harvested vegetables and fruit before they are sold, collected, or transported off site. Produce may be stored for several days, and it is essential that it is kept fresh and in good condition. The shed was constructed in late summer 2007.

By that time, the city authorities in Philadelphia had made a lot of publicity about green roofs and a new planning law had been enacted requiring green roofs on new large buildings. One of the first green roof companies to be set up in the United States, Roofscapes, Inc., is based in Philadelphia. Mary had therefore become familiar with what green roofs were all about and decided that the farm should have one. The main reason for installing the green roof was to reduce the energy costs required to power the air conditioning unit that was used to keep the refrigeration shed cool.

Designing and planning

Mary took some advice from a commercial green roof supplier, but didn't really like the look of what she saw. 'It thought it was too densely planted. I was worried about how much it would cost, and how heavy having so many plants would make it. We thought we would try and do it ourselves.'

Installation

The roof is composed of 12-mm (0.5-in) thick outdoor plywood, supported on timber joists placed about 1 m (3 ft) apart. Wooden planking was fixed to the ends of the joists all around the roof and a simple siding of 12-mm (0.5-in) ply was fixed to that to contain the green roof. A geotextile fleece was placed over the base and sides. Then a heavy-duty waterproof liner was rolled out over that, draped over three of the sides, and tacked to the outside of the siding. The siding without the liner enables water to drain from the base of the roof, and the runoff drips into a gutter, which empties into a water cistern.

There was no drainage layer. Instead, waste or used plant trays from the plant nursery on site, measuring around 0.3 × 0.6 m (1 × 2 ft), were filled with growing medium and placed on the entire roof surface. The roof is therefore a DIY version of a modular system. Mary wanted to use the trays because if there were ever a leak in the roof, she would be able to take up a tray and fix the leak without damaging the whole roof. Additional growing medium was spread over the whole roof surface, so it is not apparent that the trays are beneath. The growing medium consists of ⅓ green waste compost from the city of Philadelphia, ⅓ rock aggregate (the most lightweight pebbles that could be sourced locally), and ⅓ perlite. The green waste compost was supplemented with additional composted bark because Mary felt that the city material might have a very high pH.

The plants used in the roof are a mix of whatever was available at the nursery at the time. Black-eyed Susan (*Rudbeckia triloba*), fountain grass (*Pennisetum setaceum*), and *Sedum rupestre* are the main plants. They were spaced at around 30 cm (12 in) apart and watered once upon planting. Subsequently there has been no watering and no maintenance. The roof is remarkably free of weeds.

Success of the green roof

The roof has definitely achieved its main purpose of cutting down on energy costs. Although she has not monitored it directly, Mary can point to the difference in costs from before the roof was installed to afterwards. In August 2007, before the roof was put on, the energy cost for cooling the building was $900, whereas in July 2008 (the hottest month of the

---

The growing medium consists of one third green waste compost from the city of Philadelphia, one third rock aggregate (the most lightweight pebbles that could be sourced locally), and one third perlite.

---

year), cooling costs were $530. This reduction of over 30 percent in energy costs represents a significant and important sum for a not-for-profit organization.

The inclusion of the tall grass makes the roof very visible from ground level, giving it the appearance of a wheat field atop the building, although the grass density is quite low. Mary says that although some people come to the city farm specifically to look at the green roof, for most people it takes them by surprise, generating comments like 'Your roof sure does need a haircut.' When asked if there are any problems with the roof, Mary says there were none whatsoever. Asked what she might do differently now, Mary feels that she could perhaps have spent more effort on the sides—making them more attractive and hiding the overlapping waterproofing. 'We didn't think enough about the people who would be looking at the roof' she says.

Vegetables are grown in beds on a concrete floor. Photo by Nigel Dunnett

Salad greens are produced hydroponically. Photo by Nigel Dunnett

GREEN ROOFS
on Garages and Other Structures

The green roof covers a carport. Photo by Wendy Allen

LIPTAN GARAGE

Portland, Oregon, United States • Owner and designer: **Tom Liptan** •
Context: **Private residential** • Size: **2.5 × 6 m (8 × 20 ft)** • Main
purpose of green roof: **Stormwater management, aesthetic**

The ecoroof on the garage. Photo by Tom Liptan

No book on small-scale green roofs would be complete without including Tom Liptan's garage roof. Tom has been an inspirational figure to many in the green roof world, and he has definitely made Portland, Oregon, a world centre not just for green roof applications (or ecoroofs, as he prefers to call them), but for creative landscape-based approaches to stormwater management in general. Tom has been a pioneer and created his garage ecoroof at a time when there were few, if any, other examples of green roofs in the United States.

For more than twenty years, Tom has worked for the City of Portland on water management issues. He had some notion of green roofs from meeting and talking with European visitors, but in 1994 he had a eureka moment. 'My wife had bought some hand-wash soap, and on the label it mentioned that it was produced in Belgium in a factory with a green roof,' says Tom. He was spurred into finding out more and became fixed on the idea of trying to apply the concept himself.

Designing and planning

Tom had a garage on his lot, dating from 1919, which was at the point of falling down. In the autumn of 1995, he started on a project to install a temporary ecoroof on the garage, after which he would take the garage down and rebuild it. The garage and green roof are still there. Tom upgraded the existing garage structure, strengthened the building with additional cross supports, and replaced the rotting roof deck with new boards.

Above: The yellow tulip.
Photo by Tom Liptan

Right: *Muscari* among the
sedums. Photo by Tom
Liptan

Installation

For the green roof, Tom decided to keep things simple and to do without a drainage mat. He kept the existing single-ply bitumen waterproofing and laid a thin layer of newspaper over the top to even out the underlying surface and to help prevent any damage to the liner. He placed a flexible waterproofing liner, and then another thin layer of newspaper. Next, he added 50 mm (2 in) of growing medium, using soil from his backyard garden. The roof was then planted, mostly with sedums, but he has tried out many other plants.

Success of the green roof

Tom describes the joy and delight of watching a green roof, your own creation, evolve and change over time, each year bringing new surprises.

Unbeknownst to him, a tulip bulb was in the soil he put up on the ecoroof in 1996. Two years later he noticed a scrawny little tulip-like leaf. The next year he saw the same thing, but it looked healthier and larger. In subsequent years more leaves appeared, until finally it produced a bud about mid-March 2007. Tom wondered, 'Would it open? Every day, morning before work and evening when I returned, I looked, but it didn't open. Of course, I watched it all day on Saturdays and Sundays. Then on the morning of March 31, my daughter Liz's birthday, I gazed out the window and the flower was there, fully open, beautiful yellow in the morning sun. . . . What a joyous day—my daughter's gift to me.' In 2008 it bloomed again, and by 2010 the tulip had become five separate plants, each with a flower.

JOHNSON GARAGE

Waitakere City, Auckland, New Zealand • Owner and designer: **Doug Johnson** • Context: **Private detached garage** • Size: **90 m² (968 sq ft)** • Main purpose of green roof: **Stormwater management, aesthetic**

Doug Johnson had identified a perfect location for a new rural house on a site in the foothills of the Waitakere Ranges about a forty-minute drive north-west of Auckland, New Zealand. Strict zoning regulations prohibited building unless the amount of impermeable surface created by the new building and its driveway was offset. Creating a green roof on the main residence was thought to have a possible negative impact on the future marketability of the dwelling, but a green roof on the garage provided the opportunity to try something innovative. 'When visiting Swiss alpine areas, I saw pump sheds, barns, and wood sheds with pasture and wildflower roofs that blended into the alpine meadows,' says Doug. This prompted him to try something similar. This interest was complemented by attending a course run by the Biological Building Institute on environmentally sustainable houses. One of the tutors was Johann Bernhardt, who became the architect of the house.

Designing and planning
The green roof sits over a near-flat concrete roof deck and was designed by Doug. An EPDM liner with protective felt blanket beneath underlies a rigid plastic waffle drainage board (individual squares are clicked together) covered with a separate filter cloth. The EPDM liner runs up to the edge of the low parapet that retains the substrate. This concrete block parapet is capped with a moulded steel edging sitting on wood blocks to protect the liner from sun exposure.

Installation
The waterproof liner was installed by the construction company that developed the site and built the

The green roof was planted with colourful flowering plants.
Photo by Doug Johnson

house, and the rest of the work was done by Doug. A drought-tolerant wildflower seed mix (non-native species, mainly European) was sown. The substrate is 100 to 150 mm (4 to 6 in) deep and a blend of pumice, composted bark, and topsoil. This overlies 50 mm (2 in) of medium to fine sand. For amenity reasons, the green roof is irrigated in late summer using sprinklers until water begins to run from the roof.

Success of the green roof

A major problem arose initially as there were months of delay between spreading of the substrate and sowing of seeds due to the regulatory authority not confirming a suitable native species mix. (This was one of the very first extensive roofs in Waitakere City.)

The wildflowers are attractive and fit comfortably with the pasture and shrubland adjacent. Doug says in the future he would plant immediately after laying substrate and may sow more densely to reduce the number of weeds invading the roof. Over time he aims to replace the non-native species with native species.

When visiting Swiss alpine areas, I saw pump sheds, barns, and wood sheds with pasture and wildflower roofs that blended into the alpine meadows.

Littleborough, Lancashire, United Kingdom • Owner: **Georgina Cape** •
Designer: **Richard Storah** • Context: **Private residential, garage** • Size:
25 m² (270 sq ft) • Main purpose of green roof: **Aesthetic, stormwater
management, wildlife habitat**

GEORGINA CAPE lives in the Lancashire Pennines,
part of a chain of hills running up the spine of
northern England. The upland landscape is rugged,
with moorland, pasture and rough grassland, small
patches of woodland, rocky outcrops, and fields
divided by dry-stone walls. The weather is rugged,
too. Both winters and summers can be cold, wet, and
windy, but there can also be periods of hot summer
weather and drought. Georgina was already familiar
with green roofs—the headquarters of the German
company she works for is covered in green roofs—so
when she decided on an eco-friendly conversion of
her house, a green roof was a must-have.

Designing and planning

Before starting anything, Georgina undertook some
background research. She found the Living Roof
leaflet produced by Natural England particularly
valuable, and it convinced her that a green roof was

conceivable even in the harsh, wet, windy, and rarely
sunny conditions of the Pennines. She knew the roof
would need to include hardy plants such as sedums,
alpines, and sempervivums, but she was also very
keen to have local native plants included in the
planting. So she began to collect seeds from the surrounding landscape to compliment those that would
be planted. The main driving force behind the green
roof was the creation of a local and attractive habitat on the roof that would complement the other
features of the conversion, including the earth-
sheltered walls. However, the green roof would also
allow the property to merge with the surrounding landscape and provide some additional water
attenuation.

Richard Storah, a local architect, was charged
with the entire project. As the whole conversion
needed to gain planning permission, both the architect and the Cape household were pleased (and
relieved) that the local planners were very positive
about the application in general and specifically
the green roof. It would be the first of its kind in
the immediate local area. The green roof sits over a
garage which is built into an earthen bank, and the
roof level is the same as and directly linked to the
surrounding grassland. The garage wall is faced with

The roof joins seamlessly with the neighbouring landscape. The wire fence was added is to keep out rabbits (and cows). Photo by Dusty Gedge

natural stone, with stone coping, and reflects exactly the appearance of the local dry-stone walls.

Installation

The build-up of the roof consists of a standard extensive green roof system. A moisture blanket and drainage layer with filter sheet sits on the waterproofing, onto which 100 mm (4 in) layer of clay-fired pellet-based growing medium was laid. A local building contractor, who had never installed a green roof before, laid the waterproofing and the other engineered elements, but Georgina and the family undertook all the planting and seeding.

The roof was planted with native sedums, alpine species, and local wildflowers that were grown from seed, including small scabious (*Scabiosa columbaria*),

tormentil (*Potentilla erecta*), foxglove (*Digitalis purpurea*), clover (*Trifolium pratense*), and a few garden escapes such as *Dianthus*. The roof has a dry-stone wall boundary on one side, which creates a shady area, which has proved advantageous for the locally collected foxgloves. Rosemary (*Rosmarinus officinalis*) was also planted and appears to like the quite harsh conditions on the roof. In addition to the plants, logs and bundles of twigs were added to provide habitat as well as stony areas and an area of sand to create different substrate conditions for invertebrates.

Success of the green roof

On the infrequent sunny days of north-western England, the roof can be a real feast of activity with spiders, bees, and butterflies. Rabbits, although potentially a natural maintenance team, soon discovered the roof. They didn't cause any problems to the plants on the roof but did start digging, so a piece of chicken wire fence was built to keep the rabbits out. Another visitor, a cow, wandered onto the roof before the fence had been installed and left a trail of hoof prints as it was shooed away!

There has been about a 75 percent survival rate, which indicates that most species have more or less managed.

The garage roof is built into a hillside and is connected to the local landscape, making access very easy for maintaining and playing around with the roof. This includes the occasional weeding (once a month in summer) to take out the meadow grasses, dandelions, and tree saplings that are blown in from the surround landscape. They also apply organic chicken manure pellets as fertilizer from time to time. The roof is never irrigated because this part of England does have ample rain.

One of the slight problems with the roof has been the slower-than-expected growth of the plants. The periods of excessive heat, drought, and nearly constant rain make the conditions on the roof particularly severe. There has been about a 75 percent survival rate, which indicates that most species have more or less managed.

Georgina not only feels completely rewarded by the view and the wildlife activity, but is so relieved that she did not get bamboozled with all the technical details and expert opinions. She advises, 'Have a go, and don't get too bogged down in what the professionals think. Most of the contacts I made were sedum blanket suppliers who were either frustrating or completely unhelpful, which made us have a bash instead of doing it the "right" way.' Are there things that she would do differently next time? 'I would have grown more plants myself. I would add more contours to the finished profile of the roof instead going for a flat finish.'

The roof has been a success, and the Cape household have now gained much confidence. So much so, that they are planning another roof on a small strawbale building. The current roof is attractive and doing exactly what it was intended to do. It was also very cost effective, with a total cost around £5000 in 2005 including labour, all materials, and the drystone walling. The Cape household consider this money well spent. They have an attractive view and a lot of positive feedback from visitors and locals—including the cow.

LEWISHAM WEARSIDE DEPOT

Lewisham, London, United Kingdom • Owner: **London Borough of Lewisham** • Designer: **Grass Roof Company and Dusty Gedge** • Context: **Council depot** • Size: **70 m² (750 sq ft)** • Main purpose of green roof: **Biodiversity, water retention, water quality**

Vegetation establishment was very successful. The roofs are highly visible, promoting a lot of interest and comment. Photo by Dusty Gedge

THESE GREEN roofs were retrofitted on a small building housing a generator and two metal modular buildings situated alongside the Ravensbourne River. As the borough's biodiversity action plan—a strategy prepared by the local council to promote target species and habitats within the area—promotes the use of green roofs for biodiversity, the roofs were designed to encourage wildlife.

Nick Pond, the local nature conservation officer, had received funds to build the green roofs from the depot manager, who was keen to demonstrate that his department were taking the biodiversity action plan seriously. A further objective was to use the roofs as an example of good practice to stimulate other managers and departments to consider retrofitting small-scale green roofs on other buildings in the borough's ownership. The context of the buildings would help, too, as the conference meeting room of the neighbouring office compound overlooks the green roofs. Along with a series of small ecological improvements to the river and a small wildlife garden within the depot, the green roofs would add an additional feature for wildlife within an area that is essentially tarmac.

The project was also partly funded by the invertebrate charity Buglife. The roofs are included in a continuing project to monitor green roofs and invertebrate biodiversity undertaken by the charity with Dusty Gedge of Livingroofs.org and Dr. Gyongyver

Julia Kadas. Bimonthly visits are undertaken throughout the summer season to collect and record the species of invertebrates that colonize the roof.

Designing and planning

The blue flat-roofed modular buildings are used to store equipment and sit side by side. The other building is a simple one-storey brick blockhouse which had been constructed about twenty years before. The existing waterproofing was a standard asphalt surface. The roof has a gentle slope, and at one end the slope ends in a flat area that tended to hold rainwater and a good deal of moss had established. The building had a simple parapet cap with a zinc protection trim. It was important that the new green roofs have a good architectural feel. The Grass Roof Company was chosen because of their track record of building attractive small-scale green roofs.

Installation

A new roof plate was constructed across both modular buildings, with wooden rafters and a plywood deck which was waterproofed with a Hertalan EPDM membrane. The edge detailing was constructed of wood, and a small outlet with chains acting as downpipes was created in one of the corners near the river.

Using a simple geotextile over the membrane, two substrates were used to create a mounded terrain across the roof. The first consists of crushed ceramics (old baths, basins, and toilets) mixed with a small amount of organic green waster compost, and the second is a brick-based growing medium with a slightly higher organic content. The depth of the substrate varies from 30 to 200 mm (1.2–8.0 in). The lower areas were formed to act as a sort of riverbed meandering across the roof to the outlet. As no drainage layer was used, these lower areas would act as drainage channels allowing excess rainwater to drain from the roof. A porous pipe was placed under the substrate to provide irrigation if needed. The roof was installed in late spring, and this would provide irrigation to help the native plug plants through the first season, but only if necessary.

The first step during construction of the green roof on the brick building was to clean the waterproofing of lichen moss and the grits that had collected over time. Although the waterproofing was in

Mounds of varying depths were formed, with a simple shingle drainage channel weaving through the landscape to drain excess water.

good condition, no one could be sure that it would provide root protection. Therefore a simple EPDM pond liner was laid across the existing waterproofing to act as root barrier, which was covered in a geotextile to provide further protection and to retain some moisture.

A degree of shading is provided by a neighbouring tree, so no irrigation system was installed and a plan was created to irrigate the roof using a standard hose if and when this was deemed necessary. The growing medium is a brick-based substrate with some loam and organic material blended into the aggregate. A similar pattern like that used on the modular buildings was created. Mounds of varying depths were formed, with a simple shingle drainage channel weaving through the landscape to drain excess water.

Two planting approaches were undertaken on both roofs: use of a London living roofs mix consisting of native herbs and annuals and the planting of a range of native plugs, including sea thrift (*Armeria maritima*), lesser knapweed (*Centaurea nigra*) *Dianthus deltoides*, viper's bugloss (*Echium vulgare*), wild strawberry (*Fragaria virginiana*), ground ivy (*Glechoma hederacea*), toadflax (*Linaria vulgaris*), bird's foot trefoil (*Lotus corniculatus*), and coltsfoot (*Tussilago farfara*). A series of logs was also used to create shade and protection from the wind and to provide invertebrate nesting sites in their crevices and holes. Later, local seeds collected from the Laban Dance Centre roof were also scattered across the roofs, with bulbs of *Muscari* and *Crocus*.

One area of the generator roof was covered with some flower-rich hay cut at John Little's garden. It is hoped that this hay will provide addition habitat for bugs and act as a mulch for any seeds that have been transported with the hay.

Success of the green roof

The roofs were an instant success. Enquiries and interest have been flooding in, and it is hoped that the borough will apply for funding to repeat the exercise on several of their other modular buildings within the borough.

The roofs were watered regularly during the dry periods in May and June, but this has been minimal. The designers hope that with the depth of the substrate and the healthy appearance of all the herbs that in future years irrigation will only be used during exceptional dry periods. The only other minor issue is the presence of fat hen (*Chenopodium album*) and other weeds, which must have come in with the growing medium. A quick weeding resolved this, however, and as the other vegetation takes hold, this type of unwanted vegetation will be kept to a minimum as competition increases.

By May of the first year, the annuals were in full bloom and the native plugs had taken to the substrate and flowered. The roof has already attracted a range of wildlife, including six species of bumble bees and at least another five hymenopterans (wasps, bees, and ants). The local house sparrow population that use the bird feeder hanging from a nearby willow tree have been seen foraging up on the roofs. Perhaps the most interesting species seen on the roof is caterpillars of the toadflax brocade moth (*Calophasia lunula*). Although they munched their way through a lot of the *Linaria vulgaris*, this is a small burden to bear considering that this moth is a priority species in the United Kingdom Biodiversity Action Plan.

EAGLE STREET ROOFTOP FARMS

Brooklyn, New York, United States • Owner: **Broadway Stages** • Designer and installer: **Goode Green** • Context: **Commercial organic green roof farm** • Size: **558 m² (6000 sq ft)** • Main purpose of green roof: **Large-scale working rooftop farm**

ROOFTOP FARMS is the first commercial organic rooftop vegetable farm of its type and scale in the United States. The organization Growing Chefs is based at the farm and aims to connect people with their food through a wide range of outreach activities and regular series of workshops revolving around issues of food sourcing, food growing, and cooking. The green roof sits on top of a warehouse owned by the Brooklyn company Broadway Stages and was designed by the green roof company Goode Green.

Designing and planning
Broadway Stages was in talks with Goode Green about installing a green roof on one of their many properties. At the same time the issues of local food and urban agriculture began to gain momentum. Goode Green wanted to incorporate a large-scale food project into their work. As a result of those discussions and the good working relationship, the project developed into a full-scale urban farm. Farmers were brought in after the installation to tend to the site.

Installation
The green roof has the standard layers of materials beneath the growing medium: root barrier, protection fabric, drainage mat, and filter fabric from the green roof company Optigrun. Over the filter fabric is an engineered growing medium consisting of a lightweight aggregate and organic matter. A crane was used to lift the 90,900 kg (200,000 lbs) of growing medium to the roof's surface in a single day. The material was then spread over the roof by a team of volunteers, and the whole job took three days. Thirty food-growing beds were formed, facing north–south and measuring 1.2 m (4 ft) wide, and these were divided by a central, mulch-covered aisle. The growing medium in the beds is 100–175 mm (4–7 in) deep. A buried pipe irrigation system delivers water. The cost of the roof was $10 per square foot. Costs were kept to a minimum by the use of recycled materials to form the roof edging.

Success of the green roof
The most successful crops include tomatoes, salad greens and microgreens (lettuce and mustard greens harvested when about 25 mm [1 in] high), onions,

A beautiful, productive rooftop space. Photo by Annie Novak

and herbs. The produce is sold directly at the farm's own market and to local restaurants. The farm also runs a community-supported agriculture scheme, whereby people buy shares in the farm and in return get a regular supply of produce. Although there is an employed farm manager, much of the work is undertaken by volunteers.

'The one benefit which was much larger and astounding than we could ever have hoped for was the community involvement and excitement. Each Sunday throughout the season over fifty volunteers show up to help out. The workshops are full, and this year's new community-supported agriculture scheme has a waiting list of sixty people,' says Lisa Goode of Goode Green. The environmental benefits are obvious, but this project has done far more for advocacy and education of green roofs and local food than was initially planned.

Substrate being lifted to the prepared roof. Photo by Annie Novak

The one benefit which was much larger and astounding than we could ever have hoped for was the community involvement and excitement.

NIGEL'S NOTES

Although this project is much larger than the other projects featured in the book, the basic principles apply at any scale. The high volunteer input—both in creating the roof and in maintaining it—shows the great level of interest not only in urban food production, but in urban rooftop food production in particular. The roof has developed strong local and community links through the community-supported agriculture scheme, but also through the Growing Chefs outreach programme, providing an inspiring example of the potential of productive green roofs. Although city tap water was used for irrigation in the roof's first season, in the future the intention is to harvest rainwater in collection tanks and to use this for irrigation.

SORRILL RESIDENCE GARAGE

Northeast Derbyshire, United Kingdom • Owner and designer: **Jeff Sorrill** • Context: **Retrofit green roof on garage** • Size: **2.5 × 3.5 m (8 × 12 ft)** • Main purpose of green roof: **Aesthetic, wildlife habitat**

After plant establishment, the deeper areas can easily been seen as they have far better vegetation growth. Photo by Jeff Sorrill

JEFF WORKS as manager of The Green Roof Centre, University of Sheffield. Most of his time is spent working on large-scale commercial projects, but he had the chance to apply the principles of creating a green roof on a much smaller scale in his own home in a Sheffield suburb. The main aim for building the green roof was aesthetic, to provide a good view from the house onto a bare and plain garage roof. Jeff also wanted to provide habitat and to try out some ideas for creating a biodiversity roof.

Designing and planning

The building structure was a standard single-leaf brick-walled garage with a plywood roof, supported on joists at 35-cm (14-in) intervals. The roof had been refelted prior to constructing the green roof, but it was already showing signs of weather-induced wear. Jeff talked to both the local planning department and building control regarding permission, and both said that he did not need to make a formal application.

Installation

Although Jeff was confident that the roof was water tight, he bought a pond liner from a local garden centre to serve as additional waterproofing and a root-resistant barrier to protect the felt. After the felt layer had been swept, the liner was simply laid over the whole roof. Treated timber was then used to construct edging on three sides to prevent the growing medium slipping off the sides. An old jute-backed

The completed roof, with mounding, logs, and stones. Photo by Jeff Sorrill

carpet was placed onto the pond liner, the idea being to protect the liner from Jeff walking about during the construction phase and to retain some moisture in dry conditions. Next, 1.5 m³ (2 cubic yd) of growing substrate was lifted onto the roof by bucket and spread across the whole area. This gave an average cover of about 60 mm (2.4 in), but the depth toward the front (that is, the side with no edging)

was reduced to prevent losing substrate into the gutter. Jeff also built up two deeper ribs of substrate from the back towards the centre of the roof, with the aim of creating a range of substrate depths across the roof. Some additional features were then added, including a tree branch, some cobbles and gravel which were no longer need in the garden, and a small area of limestone dry-stone walling to mimic that found in the Peak District National Park only 8 km (5 mi) to the west of the site.

A local garden centre was offering a variety of ten semi-mature alpine and sedum plants for £10, and this seemed to be a good way of getting the vegetation underway. Ten plants of six different types were planted on the roof, in addition to a scattering of Green Roof Centre seeds. That was all that was intentionally introduced, and the roof was then left to develop on its own.

Success of the green roof

After just over a year, the roof had settled in well. The mix of alpine and meadow plants and flowers made a very attractive contrast to the surrounding urban landscape.

If Jeff were doing this project again, the main thing he would change is placing edging around all sides. Due to the reduced depth of substrate on the open side, very little has grown in this area, resulting in quite a wide area of nothing around a green mound. In addition some material has fallen into the gutter, which requires clearing out. If Jeff had put edging on all sides, he would have also put more substrate on the roof. 'It's clear that depth is king, the more I could have got up there the better it would be,' says Jeff.

It's clear that depth is king, the more I could have got up there the better it would be.

The green roof during construction, with waterproof liner, protective old carpet on top, and substrate. Photo by Jeff Sorrill

Dronfield, Derbyshire, United Kingdom • Owner and designer: **Jeff Sorrill** • Context: **Private garage** • Size: **25 m² (270 sq ft)** • Main purpose of green roof: **Biodiversity, visual interest**

Top: The edgings of railway sleepers and stone are in place, and limestone strips trace the outline of the design. Photo by Jeff Sorrill

Above: The different substrate materials were placed directly onto the waterproofing. Photo by Jeff Sorrill

THE ROOF has been retrofitted onto a double garage in a suburban housing estate. The estate was built in the 1970s to house the staff for a large bank that had been encouraged to relocate to Sheffield. The estate is riddled with footpaths, one of which passes next to the garage. As it heads away, the path rises, so people some 45 m (50 yd) away can see the roof, but those next to it cannot. 'I work with green roofs all the time, so it only seemed fitting that I have a go of one of my own' says Jeff. 'I wanted to try a lot of different substrates in the same setting, and then hopefully to create a new habitat in an environment otherwise limited to traditional gardens.'

Designing and planning

Jeff designed the roof on the back of an envelope at a green roof conference, during a presentation in German, which he was having a difficult time paying attention to. He wanted to merge different substrates and allow materials to mix but also have clearly separate types of growing medium. He also wanted to sow the same seed across the different substrates. Jeff had a lot of information at his fingertips: 'I work at the Green Roof Centre in Sheffield, it's my job to find out about green roofs.'

Installation

Jeff installed the roof himself with many trips up a ladder carrying buckets of the different materials. 'This was part of the fun of doing it and making decisions about where different materials should go,' says Jeff. The mineral felt on the roof was in fair but weathered condition, so the roof was waterproofed again with root-resistant EPDM. No drainage board, filter sheet, or moisture mat was used—substrate went directly onto the waterproofing. Jeff built up the edging to the roof with reclaimed sleepers and local stone, common in dry-stone walls in the Derbyshire countryside. Through the Green Roof Centre he had access to suppliers of several different substrates, so he bought small samples of Heather and Lavender semi-intensive and Sedum Substrate extensive from Alumasc-ZinCo, some Green Estate Ltd. substrate, and Warrior semi-intensive substrate from Petalshell Ltd. The roof also has areas of builders ballast sand and crushed limestone, which was left over from another job. The limestone made good separators for the other substrates, and Jeff used this material to trace out the initial layout on the waterproofing. Substrates were laid to varying depths ranging from 70 to 120 mm (2.8–4.8 in).

Success of the green roof

The roof is still quite young, but it has been very interesting to see how the seeds have germinated in different ways on the various substrates. The Heather and Lavender substrate (high organic matter) area has shown rapid growth with good cover. The Warrior substrate also looks to be supporting some of the species very well, but not as many as the Heather and Lavender. As expected the extensive substrates are slower to react and have less biomass.

'I love to look at it,' says Jeff. 'Visually it makes an attractive change from all the other standard grey roofs.' In most cases people who see the roof don't know what to make of it. They just like the idea and often ask if he can help them to build one. 'The only real problem,' he says, 'has been from local cats enjoying the loose materials as a toilet!'

> *Visually it makes an attractive change from all the other standard grey roofs.*

NIGEL'S NOTES

This project shows how any suitable roof in just about any context can be designed for biodiversity. Jeff's garage brings a wildlife habitat into the heart of a typical U.K. housing estate, and it looks great too! In fact it is the contrast between the normality of the surroundings and the striking design of the roof that makes it so appealing.

Hope Valley, Derbyshire, United Kingdom • Owner and designer: **Paul Thomas** • Context: **Private residential, garage roof** • Size: **5.4 × 3 m (18 × 10 ft)** • Main purpose of green roof: **Aesthetic, wildlife habitat**

THE GREEN roof was put on the concrete-panel garage to create a green space and wildlife habitat to hide an otherwise barren and ugly fibreglass corrugated garage roof at the end of the garden. The garden slopes downwards from the house, and therefore the garage roof is very visible from the windows at the back of the house.

Paul found out about green roofs by reading newspaper articles and seeing examples at trade shows he was attending through his business, which specialises in mycorrhizal systems for aiding tree establishment. Following further internet research, Paul decided to try one out for himself to see if it could be done on a budget and as an interesting project. He also wanted to see what plant community would eventually succeed without going down the usual sedum route.

Designing and planning

To make the roof as inexpensively as possible, Paul designed the roof himself. The design incorporates many aspects found on a range of websites.

Installation

The roof was a DIY job. The garage's original joists were replaced with those with a sufficient load-bearing capacity. On top of the joists was secured one layer of marine plywood to create a strong surface, and a pond liner ordered off the internet was added as a waterproof membrane. Then a layer of old carpet was added to help distribute moisture and to protect the liner. The final layer was turf that had been removed from a lawn. The turf had a high level of moss but is also quite species diverse, with plants ranging from *Rumex* to *Aquilegia* and a few *Sedum*. Broken bricks were also spread across the roof to provide extra habitats for invertebrates.

Success of the green roof

The roof has worked far better than Paul envisaged. It has not leaked and has stayed largely green since it was installed. In terms of maintenance, Paul originally thought that he would need to mow the turf, but this has not been necessary at all and the green roof has looked after itself. The vegetation has been quite colourful, and the first year it was covered in flowering sunflowers from seed dropped by birds. As expected, the sedums have thrived, but the species composition has remained quite diverse.

For Paul, the visual aspect is very appealing, and

The slope of the garden makes the green roof easily visible. Photo by Paul Thomas

it has been very interesting to watch how the plant community has grown and changed over time. Some people who see the roof love it (or the idea of it). Others, however, don't realize what it is until it's pointed out—they think the roof is actually in disrepair and not intended to be green.

The blackbirds have very much enjoyed foraging on the roof (turning over moss), and several species of birds come to bathe in a very shallow pond that was added with a bit of off-cut pond liner. Paul has also thought about running chickens on the roof, by adding a layer of buried chicken wire to stop them digging too deep, but has never taken the plunge in doing this.

The only downside Paul can think of is that sometimes the blackbirds throw bits of moss off the side, but that is not really a problem at all. He actually would not do anything different if he were to start again. 'Some people would, I expect, prefer a mix of flowering sedums, but watching the plant community change has been part of its appeal' he says. In fact, Paul is now planning to have an even larger green roof (about four times the size) at his new house, although in this case, he says, he will probably divide the roof up into several different zones to play around with the plants a little more.

ALLEN CARPORT RAIN CHAIN GARDEN

2009 RHS Hampton Court Palace Flower Show, Surrey, United Kingdom •
Designer: **Wendy Allen of Wendy Allen Designs** • Context: **Show garden** •
Size: **3 × 3 m (10 × 10 ft)** • Main purpose of green roof: **Demonstration,
aesthetic**

Drainage detail. Photo by Wendy Allen

THIS GREEN roof installation was a gold medal winner at the RHS Hampton Court Palace Flower Show in 2009 and won the Best Sustainable Garden award. It was part of a garden designed to demonstrate how a front garden could cope with flood risk zone conditions and remain aesthetically inspiring. The green roof also replaces planting area lost through the need for a parking space.

Designing and planning

The roof was designed by Wendy, with additional structural advice on joist spacing from John Little. The green-roofed carport was the first stage of reducing rainwater runoff from the roof of the main property. This feature alone meant that up to 60 percent of rainwater would be absorbed and prevented from reaching the stormwater drains, thus reducing flash flooding. Any excess water trickled down a rain chain to a water butt (cistern) which stored rainwater for reuse. The water cistern overflowed down a second rain chain into a rain garden, a shallow free-draining depression with plants tolerating a wide range of soil conditions. The roof also featured an area where water would be allowed to pool, as well as mounded substrate to increase biodiversity.

The garden was designed to demonstrate sustainable water management in a front yard space. Photo by Wendy Allen

Installation

The support structure for the roof consisted of 50 × 150 mm (2 × 6 in) Accoya timber joists at 400-mm (16-in) intervals, with two rows of bracing strips between. For the roof deck, 18-mm (0.7-in) marine ply was used. An EPDM membrane formed the water-proofing. Accoya timber planks were used as a facia around the roof edges, and 50-mm (2-in) rusted steel angle strips were used as edge detailing to tie in with other reclaimed rusted metal features in the design.

The mineral component of the substrate consisted of crushed ceramic material from bathroom basins (a very low-cost waste material aggregate) and green waste compost in a 1:1 ratio. The planting was mostly ready-grown species-diverse Green Roof mat from Lindum Turf, with additional *Galium odoratum* and *Origanum laevigatum* 'Herrenhausen', plus *Sedum* 'Red Cauli' to trail over the edges.

Success of the green roof

Although originally designed for a show garden, according to Wendy, the roof is still going strong, having been reconstructed as part of a summerhouse at Westgate Joinery's yard in Sussex. In the longer term, she would have liked to think more carefully about the edge detailing and capping, as the way it

The green roof covers a carport. Photo by Wendy Allen

was constructed for the show would mean that moisture could wick between the liner and the frame. Also Wendy is not so sure now about using the recycled crushed ceramic as part of the substrate, having subsequently heard reports of its lead content from John Little. A big success was the use of Accoya timber, which is ideally suited to green roof applications due to its inherent water-repelling properties,

durability rating, and eco credentials. As Wendy says, 'The Dutch use it to line canals with.'

At the show, Wendy fielded the most questions from the public regarding the green roof construction, and there was general amazement that the rain chain feature could so effectively replace a traditional plastic downpipe.

EMORY KNOLL FARMS SHED, OFFICE, GARDEN TRIAL ROOF, AND CAT SHELTER

Street, Maryland, United States • Owner and designer: **Edmund Snodgrass** • Context: **Equipment storage, office, trial garden structure, and cat shelter** • Size: **From 140 m2 (1500 sq ft) to 0.7 m2 (8 sq ft)** • Main purpose of green roof: **Demonstration, horticulture, experimental**

The cat shelter. Photo by Ed Snodgrass

As one might expect, Emory Knoll Farms, the first green roof nursery in North America and the major supplier of green roof plants, has several green roofs on the premises serving various functions. One of the roofs was planted on an existing structure, while the other three are new construction. They range in function from equipment storage to a shelter for an aging feline. Almost all of the construction work, with the exception of the trial garden structure, was done by the staff at Emory Knoll Farms.

Designing and planning

Ed designed and planned the roofs himself. 'I worked as a carpenter in my younger years and came from a long line of farmers and builders. We always did our own repairs on the farm.' No planning permission was needed for any of the green roofs: the

barn was a reroofing of an existing structure, the others were too small to need a permit and were unoccupied agricultural structures.

Installation

In 2005, Emory Knoll Farms decided to build an equipment shed to harbour machinery from around the nursery. Recycled arches from a greenhouse that collapsed in a snowstorm the previous year formed the backbone of the new green roof. In shape, the new green roof was intended to evoke European barrel-roofed greenhouses, with a pleasing curved line. The construction began with the digging of eight holes in two lines, into which pressure-treated 100 × 100 mm (4 × 4 in) posts were placed. The posts were tamped in with stone dust, after which the tops were notched to accommodate the main beam, which measures 5 cm × 25 cm × 3.6 m (2 in × 10 in

Far left: The green roof atop the company offices. Photo by Ed Snodgrass

Above: The completed equipment shed roof. Photo by Ed Snodgrass

Left: The equipment shed roof under construction. Photo by Ed Snodgrass

× 12 ft). The bows were attached to the beam, on top of which exterior-grade plywood was screwed, using self-tapping metal screws. The plywood thus assumed the shape of the bows. An EPDM membrane was laid on top of that, followed by a nonwoven geotextile designed to protect the membrane. On the sides of the green roof, which form a weep edge, the team used silicone caulk to bond paving stones to the EPDM membrane. On the arch ends, they used plastic recycled lumber, which provided the depth for the soil.

The green roof medium was 9 cm (3.6 in) deep and comprised expanded shale, slate, clay, and compost. The shed roof was initially planted with all South African natives: *Delosperma brunnthaleri, Delosperma aberdeenense, Delosperma ecklonis, Delosperma* 'Ouberg', *Malephora crocea* 'Tequila Sunrise', *Kalachoe thyrsiflora*, and *Delosperma cooperi*. In 2007, the roof was replanted with a new group of plants: *Sedum acre, Sedum acre* 'Oktoberfest', *Sedum aizoon, Sedum album, Sedum ellacombeanum, Sedum floriferum, Sedum hispanicum, Sedum hybridum* 'Czars Gold', *Sedum kamtschaticum, Sedum montanum, Sedum oreganum, Sedum pulchellum, Sedum reflexum, Sedum rupestre, Sedum sexangulare, Sedum sieboldii, Sedum spurium, Sedum stoloniferum, Sedum telephium fabaria, Sedum takesimense, Silene uniflora*, and *Thymus serpyllum*. This allowed for the experimentation with a new mix of plants. Also, since the farm receives many outside visitors, it provided a new surface to showcase some of the nursery's plants, as well as to trial some new plants.

A second green roof at the nursery was constructed atop the old dairy barn that now serves as the offices for Emory Knoll Farms. This roof is visited by many outside groups, including landscape architects, engineers, school and university groups, and the media. A staircase and observation deck were built to provide easy access to the green roof, which is 140 m² (1500 sq ft) on a 2:12 (10°) pitch. The structural loading of the old roof was increased with the addition of a new beam that cut the span of the rafters in half. On top of the barn's corrugated metal roof, a DensDeck insulation system was adhered with fasteners and large plastic washers, creating one continuous surface on which to work and plant. On top of the DensDeck went EPDM and then a nonwoven geotextile cloth. A 10-cm (4-in) gravel stop was screwed onto the facia board running the length of the green roof.

The team applied 10 cm (4 in) of green roof medium to the roof. The first plantings in 2002 were single-species trials of *Sedum* and *Delosperma*. In the autumn of 2007, all of the medium was stripped off and the plants removed. In its place, they put down a new expanded clay, slate, and shale medium, which was FLL (the German green roof guidelines) compliant. The intent of the second planting was to create a distinctive landscape design, which Emory Knoll Farms now evaluate periodically for design integrity and plant creep. Plants used in the second planting include numerous sedum varieties, such as *Sedum spurium* 'Schorbusser Blut', *Sedum sexangulare, Sedum kamtschaticum, Sedum reflexum, Sedum rupestre* 'Angelina', and *Sedum floriferum* 'Weinenstaphaner Gold.' The design clearly evokes moving water, an echo of a stream on the property that empties into a larger body of water.

The third green roof is 3.6 × 7.3 m (12 × 24 ft) on a 1:12 (5°) pitch. It is a freestanding structure build on a concrete base which was designed to serve as a garden trial area for nonsucculent plant varieties and different medium depths. The structure was built to specification by a local contractor, using 5 × 25 cm (2 × 10 in) beams placed at 40-cm (16-in) intervals along the 20-mm (0.75-in) plywood deck. The green roof has a TPO membrane, along with an American Hydrotech drainage layer and filter cloth. As on the other green roofs at Emory Knoll Farms, there is a gravel stop, this one 15 cm (6 in) high. The medium depth varies from 12.5 to 25.0 cm (5–10 in). Plants trialled on the roof have included over 600 varieties of herbaceous perennials plus desert annuals, South African succulents, North American natives, some tender succulents for seasonal interest, and short grasses.

The fourth green roof was designed and built by Ed Snodgrass as a structure to house an aging cat. It was constructed of scrap 5 × 10 cm (2 × 4 in) wood and plywood and was built to accommodate a 0.6 × 1.2 m (2 × 4 ft) existing green roof module, with a substrate depth of 9 cm (3.6 in). Ed used leftover house siding to construct the sides of the structure. On the ends, he used brick pavers to finish the shelter and provide a base for the module. Of the four structures, it was the easiest to build, due both to its small size and the availability of scrap materials. It's built to allow for the planted module to be lifted out and replaced as desired. The plants include *Sedum album, Sedum sexangulare, Sedum kamtschaticum, Phlox subulata, Thymus serpyllum* 'Minus', *Veronica whitleyi, Sempervivum* species, and *Penstemon pinifolius.*

GREEN ROOFS ON HOUSES

The house is covered with several different types of green roof, which are very visible to surrounding residents. Photo by Dusty Gedge

Islington, London, United Kingdom • Owner: **Justin Bere** • Designer: **Bere Architects, Kim Wilkie, and Dusty Gedge** • Context: **Residential and office** • Size: **233 m² (2500 sq ft)** • Main purpose of green roof: **Biodiversity, water retention and cleansing, food production**

Hazels (*Corylus avellana*) are planted behind a narrow woodland edge of cornfield annuals. Photo by Dusty Gedge

Hemmed in all sides by housing, The Muse was previously the home of a couple of old dilapidated factories. Justin Bere of Bere Architects had dreamed up an idea of putting soil on roofs for wildlife and farming while a child in Somerset, and this small plot of land provided him with the opportunity. He had a vision of building himself a home and office covered with plants.

Justin is a leading passive house architect in the United Kingdom, and the house has therefore been built to the highest environmental standards. Due to the nature of the passive house process, all the roofs were sturdy enough to take the loads needed for green roofs. Two stepped roofs meet at a lower court-yard roof, and another green roof sits above a small studio flat on the other side of the courtyard.

The Muse took Justin over six years to build, and one of the greatest challenges was access to the site—down a narrow gravel driveway hemmed in by build-ings. This is not the sort of terrain that allowed for cranes and other mechanical help. This had major implications when it came to installing the roofs. A lot of people-power was called for.

Designing and planning

The four green roofs all have different treatments. The roof of the studio flat was designed to create a screen, ameliorating the view of the back ends of some houses. The main central roof garden consists of a hazel grove and has a path and two patio areas made of Forest Stewardship Council–certified decking. Hidden within the grove is a series of bird feeders, and several nest boxes have been installed in the garden wall. Above the main office is a relatively large meadow roof, and Justin designed the upper roof to be a dry meadow. This upper roof currently houses a solar thermal panel, and there are plans to add another one later. All the roofs have additional features, including old logs in the hawthorn copses, hazel grove, and meadow. A long mound of coarse sand has been added at the back end of the meadow to provide potential nesting habitat for burrowing bees.

Installation

The under-layers consist of a 25-mm (1-in) drainage layer with filter sheet on mastic asphalt. Although this was relatively easy to install, the greatest challenge in the construction was getting the growing medium up onto the roofs. Delivery access was tight but the growing medium was offloaded as close to the roofs as possible. More than 200 25-L (5.5-gallon) bags of the two growing media were delivered, and these had to be carried up onto the roof. The first stage from ground to the lower roof used a mechanical elevator device, and then a team of five people including Dusty Gedge, Justin, and Molly Stroyman (a visiting green roofer from Canada) distributed the bags to the various roofs. All in all, it took a whole day to get the soils in place and the vegetation planted.

The planting of the studio green roof was recommended by landscape architect Kim Wilkie to consist of hawthorn copses underplanted with mullein (*Verbascum thapsus*) and foxglove (*Digitalis purpurea*). The hazel grove of the main central roof is underplanted with Solomon's seal (*Polygonatum multiflorum*), wood spurge (*Euphorbia amygdaloides*), and dog's mercury (*Mercurialis perennis*), and clematis has been planted along the garden wall. A further feature at this level is a wonderful *Wisteria* tree that spills out over the roof garden. There are plans to train this to create a vegetated shelter to retire to when the sun is at its peak. The substrate used for both of these roofs consists of an intensive aggregate-based growing medium at a depth of 300 mm (12 in).

Above the main office is a relatively large meadow roof, consisting of an extensive green roof substrate at an average depth of 100 mm (4 in), but with areas mounded to create some topography to support plants that need a slightly greater depth. The roof was planted with thirteen species of native wildflowers and some *Sedum acre* and *Sedum album*. The native herbs included sea thrift (*Armeria maritima*), wild basil (*Clinopodium vulgare*), maiden pink (*Dianthus deltoides*), viper's bugloss (*Echium vulgare*), rockrose (*Helianthemum nummularium*), bird's foot trefoil (*Lotus corniculatus*), marjoram (*Origanum majorana*), and tufted vetch (*Vicia sativa*). The roof was also seeded with a wildflower mix including native annuals.

The substrate depth of the dry meadow on the upper roof is not more than 100 mm (4 in). No planting was done on this roof; it was seeded with a green roof mix devised by Nigel Dunnett. It is quite evident that the plants are more successful under the solar panels, as they are shaded and rainfall runs out of the evacuated tubes onto the plants.

These green roofs are inaccessible and planted to attract wildlife. Photo by Dusty Gedge

Success of the green roof

The Muse has been featured in many magazines and television programmes, and it received international coverage when a beehive was installed on the roof in the summer of 2009. It is at the local scale, however, that the impact of the roof can be measured—in terms of the response of neighbours and the wildlife that the roof has attracted. Overlooked by more than twenty properties, local residents regale with tales of how their lives have been enriched with the creation of the oasis that they look out on. Justin has watched and photographed a whole range of birds on the roof, including goldfinches and house sparrows feeding among the hawthorn and hazel and on the seeds of plants in the meadow. Butterflies, such as the small blue, have been seen feeding on the meadow, and many different bees and other insects have been recorded on the roof.

New York City, United States • Owner and designer: **Chris and Lisa Goode** • Context: **Private rooftop residence** • Size: **560 m² (6000 sq ft)** • Main purpose of green roof: **Aesthetic, recreation, food production**

The lower level intensive lawn. Photo by Lisa Goode/Goode Green

CHRIS AND Lisa own a building in Manhattan and live in the rooftop penthouse apartment. In fact, they were the developers and contractors responsible for the development of the whole building, and they investigated the possibility of a green roof as part of that development. With buildings being so densely packed in Manhattan, and land prices being so high, rooftops often represent the only opportunity for outdoor garden space. Rather than incorporate a traditional roof garden, Chris and Lisa wanted to apply the more sustainable ideas embedded in green roofing principles to the creation of a primarily recreational space.

Designing and planning

'Because this was a DIY project and we didn't know too much about green roofs, the learning curve was steep,' says Lisa. They sourced materials and soil samples, and designed the garden themselves. The soil depths range from 100 to 750 mm (4–30 in).

There are intensive areas of planting such as the rose bed and hornbeam hedge. Extensive areas include a lawn and a sedum and wildflower expanse. Chris and Lisa wanted a green roof because they thought it would be much more dynamic than the conventional

Every spare inch of space has been greened on the roof of Lisa and Chris's building. Photo by Lisa Goode/Goode Green

alternatives, but also because of its environmental benefits and much greater design flexibility. Lisa did a good amount of background research. 'At the time, there were no companies in New York City to talk to, so we spoke with everyone from Emory Knoll Farms to Rooflite.'

Installation

Chris and Lisa took on the green roof as another facet of the construction. They got a crane to hoist the super sacks of medium, but laid the materials and planted themselves. A high-quality loose-laid rubber roof was installed in conjunction with a leak-detection system. On top of that, rigid insulation, fabrics, drainage mat, and growing medium layers were placed, according to a standard green roof build-up.

Success of the green roof

Lisa says, 'We did this in 2004, when we had little experience of green roofs, and neither did many

A beautiful flowering meadow on the top level extensive roof.
Photo by Lisa Goode/Goode Green

other people in the United States. The green roof base is a mix of products that we now don't prefer. The products and our knowledge have improved since then.' Despite that, Lisa and Chris are very happy with the roof. Most plants adapt very well to the engineered medium. The plants that don't succeed seem to have more to do with site conditions (heat and wind) than because of failures in the green roof technology. Perhaps surprisingly, the big success is the lawn—it needs very little watering. This is due

in part to the green roof build-up, but also because the pitch of the roof allows for the drainage mat to catch water from other more irrigated areas.

'We intended to build a haven where we could enjoy the outdoors in an urban setting. We not only have that but we grow vegetables, raise chickens, and help to combat environmental issues,' enthuses Lisa.

One of the outstanding aspects of the green roof is its comprehensive use of the rooftop space to create a truly multifunctional garden area. As such, the green roof provokes a huge amount of interest. 'One comment we get a lot is that the garden doesn't feel like a rooftop. I think using even less decking would have carried this illusion further. We have areas of gravel and brickwork and a lot of plants that aren't typical to roof gardens,' says Lisa. Indeed, the level of support and excitement from people who see the green roof has been so great that in 2008 Lisa and Chris started their own business, Goode Green, specializing in innovative, exciting, and carefully designed multifunctional rooftop spaces.

We intended to build a haven where we could enjoy the outdoors in an urban setting. We not only have that but we grow vegetables, raise chickens, and help to combat environmental issues.

London, United Kingdom • Owner and designer: **David Matzdorf** • Context: **Private residential** • Size: **15 × 5.5 m (50 × 18 ft)** • Main purpose of green roof: **Aesthetic, biodiversity, horticultural experimentation**

INSTALLING A green roof was a great benefit in persuading the local authority to grant planning consent for the house. The roof is on a new residence on a very small infill site in central London, with very strict controls on the type, character, and amount of new-build possible in an established neighbourhood. To minimize visibility from the street, one of the planning conditions imposed was that the west end of the house (the most visible) could only be one storey high, and the east end two stories. The architect Jon Broome came up with the solution of a curved roof linking the two stories, upon which the green roof was installed.

A further planning constraint was that the building had to be set 5 m (16 ft) back from the road. This tiny area became the only available space for a garden on the ground. By designing a visible and accessible green roof with a good range of plants, the effective garden space available to David, a keen horticulturist, was doubled.

Finally, David wanted to take advantage of all the potential ecological and environmental benefits that green roofs offer. A particular interest was to attempt to create a roof with significant biodiversity potential, but planted predominantly with exotic or garden plants. He saw the roof mainly as an experiment, to see which plants succeeded and which failed in this inner-city site, which benefited from London's urban heat island and which might therefore enable relatively tender or less hardy plants to survive, compared with other areas in the United Kingdom.

Designing and planning

The low-tech approach to the structure and the substrate was worked out in conjunction with the architect Jon Broome and the contractor Martin Hughes, as an integral part of the design of the house. The design of the planting and the selection of species is entirely David's, although he corresponds daily with horticulturalists all over the world. The planting scheme has devised over time and is still developing, starting with the obvious *Sedum* species and experimenting from there with ever more far-fetched candidates.

Installation

The green roof was installed as part of the main contract to build the house. David was part of the work

The green roof is on a curved sloping roof, which creates a range of moisture regimes from top to bottom. Photo by Jane Sebire

team when the substrate was installed. The timber house and roof use breathing-wall construction. Over the main roof deck is a welded PVC membrane (Kaliko), with building textile laid over that. A lattice of 25 × 50 mm (1 × 2 in) unpreserved timbers was laid on the sloping areas of roof to prevent the soil from slumping in its first few years, until the plant roots had stabilized it. A leaky-pipe irrigation system was run under the soil along these timbers. The 100-mm (4-in) depth of sieved sandy loam soil was laid on the roof, and a coir mat, normally used for sand dune erosion control, was tied to the timbers and fixed over the soil. There is no dedicated drainage layer—about 70 percent of the roof slopes, so it is not really necessary except at the top, where the roof is flat. No specially formulated green roof substrate was used; the soil was sourced by the contractor from an unknown source.

Planting was done using individual plugs and pot-grown plants. A flap was cut in the coir mat (which

Right: The house sits in a very constricted urban space in London. Photo by Jane Sebire

Below: The roof resembles a Mexican hillside, with succulents and spiky agaves. Photo by Jane Sebire

decayed as planned over the course of about five years), then a small area of soil was excavated and drainage material and/or organic material was incorporated, depending on the species to be planted. Finally, the flap of mat was tucked back into the hole, while adding back the amended soil and planting out.

Success of the green roof

There have been many individual successes and failures with plants, but David's intention was to experiment, so that's to be expected. The roof has given David a horticultural challenge and a place to experiment, while providing a garden space and ecological benefits. The plant choices encourage biodiversity and demonstrate what David suspected when he started, which is that it is possible (indeed easy) to create a biodiverse green roof using predominantly exotic species.

David's speciality has been to try out a wide range of spiky South American and South African agaves, aloes, and related species. These bold plants provide a striking visual contrast to the usual lower growing or carpeting species. The free-draining soil on the sloping parts of the roof suits these species well, as they would fail in continuously damp soil in the relatively mild and wet winters of the United Kingdom. A particular success has been *Fascicularia bicolor*, a South American bromeliad (a plant which grows naturally without soil on trees). To create seasonal highlights, David grows several small shrubs on the roof, including the Mediterranean *Cistus*, and a self-seeded *Leycesteria formosa* has been allowed to stay.

The green roof keeps the house cooler in summer, especially when drought requires the occasional use of the irrigation system (which gets used, on average, four or five times per year for about twenty minutes at a time). It does not keep the house warmer in winter, however, as the soil is always damp during the cold season, and damp soil is not much use as thermal insulation.

David stresses that this is not a roof terrace. 'I don't go up there with a glass of wine and sit on a deck chair with a sun hat pulled down over my eyes—all of which would be rather difficult to haul up the ladder anyway, and it would also breach the

David's speciality has been to try out a wide range of spiky South American and South African agaves, aloes, and related species.

terms of the planning consent. It's a garden, not a patio. But I go up there most dry days between spring and autumn, just to garden and observe the plants,' says David.

Generally people who see the green roof react with astonishment—from those outside horticulture, that it should exist at all, and from those inside horticulture, that it should be possible to grow such a range of species in a 100-mm (4-in) depth of soil. David also says that the roof has been a very good way to meet his neighbours.

If David were to start again, there are several things that he would do differently. He would use better-drained soil, and a soil that was lower in nutrients to deter perennial weeds and lawn grasses, all of which colonize the roof in abundance. The flat area at the top of the roof is very difficult to manage: too wet in winter, bone-dry in summer, the soil too shallow, and the whole aspect rather shady. This area should have been laid to fall and had a deeper substrate. David is also cautious about using highly invasive plants. The worst offender has been periwinkle (*Vinca major*). Other invasive plants, such as chives (*Allium schoenoprasum*) and *Viola labradorica*, have, after two or three years of taking over the universe, settled down to their place in the overall balance of the roof, but not *Vinca major*, which continually threatens to take over the whole roof.

NIGEL'S NOTES

David's house is truly unique. He has not let himself be bound by the conventional wisdom of what a green roof should be or what plants should be successful on a green roof. Instead, he has turned his contemporary house roof into a living experiment.

Northwest London, United Kingdom • Owner and designer: **Wendy Allen of Wendy Allen Designs** • Context: **Private residential, green roof terrace** • Size: **6 × 5 m (18 × 15 ft)** • Main purpose of green roof: **Recreational space, wildlife habitat**

AS A GARDEN designer, Wendy specializes in sustainable residential gardens, often incorporating green roofs. She recognizes what perfect solutions green roofs are for many urban issues. 'The question is not why would you, but why wouldn't you,' she says.

Designing and planning

Outdoor space in London is a precious commodity, and this terrace was designed as a hybrid between an extensive green roof and a terrace area with seating. The usual solution for a roof terrace is to use plants in containers and raised beds, an intensive type approach that requires continued irrigation in summer and some degree of maintenance. There is often a preponderance of hard surface on a roof terrace, and limited biodiversity value. The solution in this case was to use extensive green roof techniques—shallow, lightweight substrates and continuous areas of drought-tolerant, low maintenance vegetation—to

The vegetation was installed using a species-rich green roof mat produced by Lindum Turf. Photo by Wendy Allen

create an attractive recreational space that also had significant attraction for wildlife. Contemporary slatted wooden screens allow light in and provide the ideal wind break ratio of 60 percent solid to 40 percent gaps, to filter the wind rather than block it. Ivy

The completed roof. Photo by Wendy Allen

boundary screens are excellent lightweight structures for an urban setting, giving year-round low-maintenance screening.

Installation

A waterproofing layer was installed over the roof structure, along with putting in a couple of replacement 50 × 100 mm (2 × 4 in) joists, new insulation, and a marine plywood roof deck. All other work,

including planting and carrying many 25-kg (55-lb) bags of substrate up the stairs, was done as a self build. The substrate was spread over a drainage layer with built-in fleece and filter layer. Western red cedar decking panels were inset and rest on the drainage layer.

Substrate depth was 100–150 mm (4–6 in) and consisted of commercial crushed-brick-based growing medium with around 15 percent organic matter.

The vegetation was established using a pregrown mat of diverse vegetation, supplied by Lindum Turf. This mat, which uses the same principles of ready-made vegetation commonly applied to sedum green roofs, consists of drought-tolerant perennials, alpines, and some sedums. The vegetation is ideally suited to green roof conditions, but gives both greater ecological and visual diversity than sedums alone. In addition, drought-tolerant perennials, herbs, and grasses are planted in these two substrates, and vegetables are grown in containers.

The vegetated areas have received no maintenance over the two-year life of the roof and have remained green and lush, despite two colder-than-average winters in London during that time.

Success of the green roof

According to Wendy, the roof has become a fabulous oasis: 'We've noticed an increase in wildlife on the roof, including birds collecting nesting material from the dead flower stalks in spring despite the fact that it is used as a recreational space.' The vegetated areas have received no maintenance over the two-year

life of the roof and have remained green and lush, despite two colder-than-average winters in London during that time.

Wendy admits that she pushed it a bit with the weight loadings, as the joists were at 500 mm (20 in) intervals and only 50 × 100 mm (2 × 4 in) in dimension. She says, 'With hindsight and knowing more now about imposed loads, I should have replaced the joists with something more substantial at the time the waterproofing was done.' Additionally, she would use the more sustainable plywood substitutes that are now available rather than marine plywood on future roof decks.

NIGEL'S NOTES

Wendy has taken an approach that points the way forward to a more sustainable means of making urban roof gardens. By using green roof ideas and thinking, she has made a very green roof terrace that does not need great inputs of water, fertilizer, or maintenance in the way that traditional roof gardens do.

FOULTON HOUSE EXTENSION

Sheffield, United Kingdom • Owner and designer: **Ben and Charlotte Foulton** • Context: **Private residential** • Size: **4 × 10 m (13 × 33 ft)** • Main purpose of green roof: **Biodiversity, visual, horticulture, insulation, cooling, noise reduction, water retention**

WHEN BEN and Charlotte put a single-storey extension at the back of their house into their small urban garden, they did not originally plan for a green roof on the building. 'The architect first designed a lead roof,' says Ben, 'but we thought this would be too expensive and would get stolen. Zinc or felt were offered as alternatives, but these were not attractive. I liked the idea of a green roof but thought it would be too difficult or expensive.'

Ben thought more about it, however, and contacted Green Estate Ltd., a Sheffield-based green roof company, for some advice and general information. He realized that a green roof would not necessarily be either costly or difficult. In reality it was the best solution, with all the added value and benefits.

Designing and planning

Once he had the confidence to go ahead, Ben mainly designed the roof himself, while discussing the materials required with Green Estate. Once the plans were completed, he went to the local council for planning approval and was asked to get a structural engineer to approve the loadings involved. Rather than rainwater runoff from the house roof going straight into the drainage system, it spills onto the gently sloping green roof of the extension, providing additional water for the vegetation, as well as stormwater attenuation for the house.

Installation

As the roof deck, 18-mm (0.7-in) plywood was used over the joists, and a breathable membrane normally used on tiled roofs was placed on top. The edgings comprised 50 × 100 mm (2 × 4 in) timber painted with bitumen. Three layers of moisture-proof membrane were laid for water and root proofing. Ben then placed plastic tanking membrane (left over from the work on the house) with blisters turned upside down for water retention. Landscape fabric was laid over the top, and then 100 mm (4 in) of Green Estate green roof substrate was added. The roof was seeded with Pictorial Meadows Green Roof seed mix (developed in association with The Green Roof Centre, University of Sheffield).

Ben assembled all the layers for the roof and put them together with the joiner who was working on the extension. 'A landscaper friend came to seed the

Ben with his extension roof. The downpipe from the roof gutter empties directly onto the green roof, providing additional water when it rains. Photo by Green Estate Ltd.

roof for me as I was a bit unsure about the planting,' he says.

Success of the green roof

After three growing seasons, Ben reports, 'I'm very happy with it—it is doing everything it should do now. No problems except it is difficult to dig into if you want to add more plants. However, I am advised to add more substrate for new planting if required.'

The room below the green roof is very cool in the summer, considering it is south facing with lots of windows. Ben says, 'My wife thinks I am a bit sad, as I get up every morning to look out of my window at my green roof. But it is just great to have this incredibly diverse and unspoilt garden!'

The vegetation on this south-facing sloping roof

Top left: Edge detail. Photo by Green Estate Ltd.

Left: The difference in vegetation from top to bottom is clear. The whole roof was originally seeded with the same seed mix, containing both herbs and sedums. Photo by Green Estate Ltd.

Above: Where water spills onto the roof from the downpipe, the vegetation is more lush. Photo by Green Estate Ltd.

has developed a distinct pattern. At the top of the roof (the very driest part), only sedums survive, and there is also a higher proportion of bare substrate. Over much of the rest of the roof, however, a more diverse mix of sedums and herbs remains. The vegetation is also very lush around the point at which the drainage downpipe spills onto the roof.

Ben says he was glad to have persevered early on. But building a green roof was definitely something he had to make an effort to find out about. 'If starting again, I might use different products on the market. It is a new technology, and there does not seem to be a central point for information. It is not something you can just ask your builder to do.'

NIGEL'S NOTES

This example shows that, even if someone is very keen to have a green roof, it can be a daunting prospect, and it is very easy to be put off by scare stories or perceived problems or expense. For a new build, where the green roof can be designed in at the start, it should be possible to achieve an excellent, cost-effective solution, especially, if as Ben did, some good advice and support can be found locally.

HANGINGWATER HOUSE

Nether Green, Sheffield, United Kingdom • Owner and designer: **Carolyn Butterworth** • Context: **Private residential** • Size: **90 m² (968 sq ft)** • Main purpose of green roof: **Biodiversity, stormwater control, protecting flat roof membrane**

The green roof. Photo by Carolyn Butterworth

CAROLYN FIRST heard about green roofs in detail in 1992 after reading an article in *Building Design* on Dusty Gedge's work with rubble roofs in Deptford in London. She then joined Sheffield's Green Roof Forum, a body within the city that comprises individuals and organizations interested in promoting and advancing green roof infrastructure within the city.

Carolyn is an architect with her own practice, and she teaches architecture at the University of Sheffield. In 2006 she received planning permission to build a new house for her family on a 14 × 30 m (45 × 100 ft) parcel of land. The brownfield site had formerly been a kitchen garden with orchard, greenhouses, joinery workshop, and garages. The site was surrounded by Victorian housing and apartment blocks and had many neighbours who looked directly down onto the plot. When she bought the parcel, all the former buildings had been demolished and the site was very overgrown. All the demolition material had been left

on site, so there was a lot of brick and concrete rubble in the top layer of the soil.

Carolyn didn't want to cart all the demolition material off to landfill and instead planned to use the rubble from the site as the growing medium for the roof. The site was full of wildlife, and she wanted to maintain this as much as possible. 'In my practice and teaching I encourage the use of non-gadgety environmentally sustainable technologies, and green roofs interest me because they are integral to a building and offer so many benefits,' says Carolyn. This was the perfect opportunity to try one out on a house.

Above: The green
roof is on top of the
house. Photo by
Carolyn Butterworth

Left: The original
rubble-covered
site of the house.
Photo by Carolyn
Butterworth

Designing and planning

The green roof was part of a sustainable design for the entire house, including high levels of insulation, air-tight construction, a mechanical ventilation and heat recovery system, air source heat pump, and underfloor heating. Carolyn worked with the green roof company Alumasc, a U.K. affiliate of the German green roof company ZinCo, on the detail of the build-up for the rubble roof, and with the help of a structural engineer she designed the roof herself.

Installation

On site, certain details were worked out with the main building contractor, Goldwing Development. The specialist subcontractor, Martin Brooks Roofing, installed a standard commercial green roof build-up, handling waterproofing of the roof and laying the drainage layer. Then Goldwing installed the growing medium consisting of demolition material and soil from the site.

Carolyn seeded the roof with a green roof mix from the Green Roof Centre, Sheffield. This is a diverse mix of species, including sedums such as *Sedum album*, *Sedum acre*, and *Sedum reflexum*, some native wildflowers, and other perennial species for summer flowering, such as *Dianthus carthusianorum* and *Petrorhagia saxifraga*.

Success of the green roof

According to Carolyn the green roof has worked very well. 'There are no problems as such, and we had a lovely display of wildflowers in the first summer.' The gravel borders need weeding three or four times a year, and wildflower seeds blow into the garden below and need weeding out, but this is a minor problem. The roof plants have survived through very hot dry conditions in the first May and June and very wet conditions in the late summer and through winter. Rainwater runoff is slow and takes three or four days to stop after a rain, which shows how effective the roof is. But the roof is not useable due to planning conditions. 'We would be overlooking the neighbours' gardens if we were up there all the time, and we don't really get the visual benefit of it either, which is a shame. . . . The neighbours like it and tell us what's growing up there.'

Carolyn has had lots of interest from students, other architects, and clients who are considering a green roof. She notes that a very good way to persuade clients that it's a reasonable option is to show them the green roof on her own house.

If Carolyn were to do it again, she would have tried to make the roof more accessible or at least more visible from inside the house or garden. 'We have to go up a ladder to see it or visit one of our neighbours' houses and look down on it,' she says.

NIGEL'S NOTES

Carolyn's use of the soil from the garden, rescued when the house was being built, as the green roof substrate goes right back to the techniques used for the original Scandinavian turf roofs, which used soils and vegetation from the exact place where the building was constructed.

KLECHA HOUSE EXTENSION

Grays, Essex, United Kingdom • Owner: **Andrew and Sue Klecha** • Green roof consultant: **John Little** • Context: **Private residential** • Size: **5 × 5 m (16 × 16 ft)** • Main purpose of green roof: **Cooling, biodiversity, aesthetic**

ANDY AND Sue have a love of food growing, and Andy was a key figure in saving their local allotment from developers over fifteen years ago. Andy works as a tree surgeon and gardener, and both he and Sue volunteer for their local Wildlife Trust.

The Klechas bought their 1930s semi-detached house in Grays, Essex, in 2000. There was a make-shift lean-to on the back of the house that was falling down and blocked the light to the small kitchen and dining area. It was obvious to them both that this needed replacing to give them extra light and space. In 2002 Andy and Sue started work on a single storey house extension to the rear of their property. They knew they did not want a conventional tiled or felt roof. After seeing some work of their friend John Little, a partner in the Grass Roof Company, they were keen to install a living roof. They loved the idea that the plants would cool their new building and bring the garden right up under their daughters' bedroom window.

Designing and planning

A simple lightweight sedum roof was specified and the plans were duly sent to the local authority for planning approval. This was where the fun started. For some reason the local authority were under the misconception the roof was for recreational use, despite the 7° pitch. After many months of John and Andy providing information on the benefits and virtues of a green roof, it took a site visit from the planners to realize the roof was there for the benefit of wildlife and the neighbours view and not to sun-bathe. Andy found this fight to get the roof disap-pointing, as he was expecting to be congratulated on his efforts to green the addition to his house and add to the biodiversity of the neighbourhood.

The Klechas had always wanted a sedum-based system, as Andy liked the idea of a 'stressed roof' and the challenge and contrast this roof would present from a horticultural perspective. They decided to use 80 mm (3.2 in) of pumice as a growing medium on top of the geotextile used to protect the liner. This was not the most sustainable substrate, but it did give the roof a lightweight, low-nutrient base, while being much more substantial than the common sedum-mat-based systems that are laid over very shallow or no substrate layer. It would allow Andy to add plants to the roof and provide lots of space for invertebrates.

Logs and pebbles add variety and interest. Photo by Jane Sebire

Using pumice also meant there was no need for a separate drainage layer.

Installation

Despite the start, Andy and Sue were still very enthusiastic to install their roof. The Grass Roof Company had used one-piece butyl rubber liners, prefabricated offsite, for small-scale roofs, so suggested this as the easiest option for Andy, who was to do most of the work himself. The roof had one drainage outlet and two Velux windows, which meant Andy and John had to be particularly careful with the measurements they provided the fabricators. With some persuasion, the liner was fitted over the Velux and down through the outlet hole cut in the roof deck, with enough excess to go up and under the lead flashing against the house. Next, a geotextile layer was added and then the 80 mm (3.2 in) of pumice substrate. The sedum blanket was laid on top of the substrate, and additional sedum and herb plugs were added to the plant mix. The total cost of the roof, materials only, was £1280 in 2002.

Success of the green roof

The first few years produced carpets of flowers from the sedums, but as the nutrients were gradually washed from the planting the roof appeared sparser and the flowering became more sporadic and patchy. Andy is very happy with this gradual change and feels the species diversity is as abundant as the original planting. He says, 'I love the challenge of establishing plants on the roof; the arid conditions really contrast to those in the garden.' The roof continues to drift through many shades of red and green and has flowered consistently.

The area where the top of the green roof meets the house is particularly dry, but this lack of plants gives sparrows a place to enjoy a dust bath. Andy has also added river pebbles, logs, and clay pots to fill some of the gaps in the plants and provide microhabitats.

Andy and Sue have already noticed new fungi and mosses appearing on the log piles as well as many other visitors. Over the years, they have also spotted bees, butterflies, and spiders, with starlings coming to root around for food. Doves and sparrows come for seeds, and many birds bring their young to hunt for insects.

The roof has never been watered and has only been fertilized occasionally with blood, fish, and bone meal. This has meant the sedums still dominate the roof and grasses have failed to establish. Andy has pulled some weeds and removed a few tree seedlings planted by the squirrels. He says, 'I add seasonal stuff like spider plants (*Chlorophytum comosum*), and other than that I keep an eye on the roof from the safety of the bedroom window!'

'It's a shame people don't get a chance to see green roofs up close. It's at that level where things really happen. We take visitors to see the roof from the upstairs windows, and they are always intrigued and

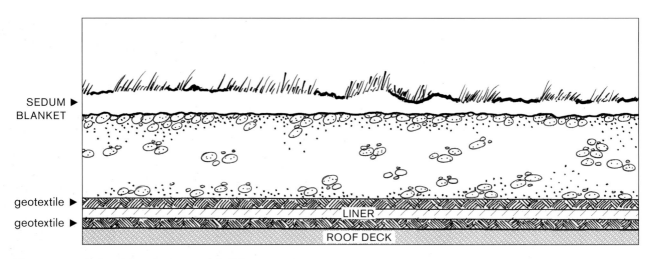

SEDUM ▶
BLANKET

geotextile ▶
geotextile ▶

LINER

ROOF DECK

The green roof build-up. Drawing by Evangelia Bakratsa

Left: Andy with the roof. Photo by Jane Sebire

Below left: The sedums provide a variety of colours and textures. Photo by Jane Sebire

Below: The view of the green roof from inside the house. Photo by Jane Sebire

surprised by the roof, and many are really enthusiastic. The local press did a piece, but this hasn't translated into more living roofs around us. We really thought ours would kick start green roof home extensions.'

The only change Andy would make, if he could, would be to bring the roof lower to get it closer to people, maybe design in viewing access. The Klechas say, 'Just do it. It's much easier than you think!'

The surplus sedum blanket from the house roof was used to make a green roof on the children's playhouse. Photo by Jane Sebire

JOHN'S NOTES

This an interesting roof. I would be keen to add some areas of deeper substrate to give a wider range of plants a chance to colonize the roof, but Andy is a patient guy and is happy to work with the pumice as his growing medium. The roof seems to have a stable plant community and requires little maintenance, so for these reasons alone it is a very valid roof. I have to be careful not to constantly strive for plant diversity when roofs like this have relevance over the long term.

I also like the way the Klechas used the surplus sedum blanket to clad the roof of their daughters' playhouse. They have grown it on two layers of upturned turf and secured it with chicken wire. Of all the green roof images I have, this is the one the magazines and media love. Maybe it's the accessibility of the roof at this level or the Hansel and Gretel appeal of the pin cushion roof.

When I look at Andy and Sue's roof, though, I still cannot understand why not one other house extension in the area has followed their lead.

TAYLOR AND GRIFFITHS ECO-HOUSE

Geraldine, South Canterbury, New Zealand • Owner: **Rhys Taylor and Anne Griffiths** • Designer: **Roger Buck Associates** • Context: **Private residential, earth-sheltered building** • Size: **85 m² (915 sq ft)** • Main purpose of green roof: **Aesthetic, nature conservation, biodiversity, waterproofing protection, insulation**

THE HOUSE, the first phase of which was constructed in 2007, is on a 6-ha (15-acre) rural site on the edge of the township of Geraldine. A primary reason for the roof was aesthetic. The beautiful scenery of the Four Peaks to the west prompted Rhys and Anne to opt for a low-profile construction to protect their eastern neighbours' views past the house. The completed house is invisible to them.

The house is built on a sloping site, and having the green roof allowed the entire east wall to be built into a hillside, creating a warm north (sun-facing) courtyard. A north-facing clerestory window coming up through the roof assists with year-round solar gain, which is maintained by high levels of

The poured concrete slab roof ready to receive the green roof. Photo by Rhys Taylor

The completed roof links the house seamlessly with the surrounding spectacular landscape. Photo by Rhys Taylor

insulation. The house is compact and approximately square, comprising a single bedroom, shower room/toilet, galley kitchen, and lounge, and a covered outside area with a workshop and carport. The house has high thermal mass, including concrete ceilings, double-paned windows, and locally designed active solar air heating and water heating equipment, and won regional energy efficiency and sustainability awards for the builders, Henderson Building.

But Rhys and Anne, as keen gardeners, also saw the roof as a botanical and ecological experiment, using only native New Zealand plants. They wanted the roof to provide food and habitat for skinks. 'We have no cat, so these native lizards are still common here,' says Rhys. The roof is accessible, and they can walk on it to observe the plants close up. The green roof was also included to give long-term protection to the waterproof membrane and to improve insulation for heat and sound.

Rhys and Anne first became aware of green roofs because a neighbour had a Swiss-style sloping turf roof. They also read about green roofs elsewhere in New Zealand, including an experimental one at Tamaki campus, Auckland.

Designing and planning

'Getting the green roof was easy. We asked for it, and it interested our architect and engineer,' says Rhys. A massive reinforced concrete structure was proposed to provide high thermal mass, and the natural ground level at the eastern end carries over the roof. The rear wall of the house is buttressed, water-proofed, insulated, and shingle drained.

Installation

The roof was built by the contractor with the rest of the house. The roof is a concrete deck. The roof panels were precast, and a top layer of concrete was poured on site. The poured concrete included a proportion of fly ash waste from steel-making to reduce its embodied energy compared to cement.

The build-up of the roof above the deck includes polystyrene insulation, a butynol waterproofing sheet brought up to a surrounding timber parapet (capped with metal flashing), a load-bearing drainage mat, geotextile as a root barrier, a layer of shingle, and a second geotextile. The substrate consists of a layer of local screened soil, topped with a thin layer of local river gravel as erosion protection. The roof is edged by paving slabs, placed edge to edge with a dished shape to channel storm water to drains which supply a stormwater holding tank.

New Zealand native plants were difficult to source. After more than a year of trying to locate them, Rhys and Anne got the help of botanists who provided propagation material from their garden collections. From a shortlist of forty species, they located samples of thirty species, and of those about twenty survive.

Success of the green roof

There was some soil and gravel movement in the early weeks, but this soon stabilized. Both weeds and planted species established rapidly in the substrate. As a result, the roof has required significant hours of weeding, especially in the first eighteen months, to get the target species established. Rhys and Anne did not water the green roof so that the desired native plants would gain an advantage over the weedy colonizers, many of which are non-native invaders. The most successful plant has been Banks peninsula blue fescue (*Festuca coxii*) which is covering the roof and invading the gravel paths and parking space surrounding the building.

In addition to the benefits of heat and sound insulation, Rhys and Anne find that the roof provides a

Rhys and Anne, as keen gardeners, saw the roof as a botanical and ecological experiment, using only native New Zealand plants.

different habitat and microclimate from the adjacent gardens on clay soil, enabling them to grow a whole different range of plants.

Visitors who see the roof are very positive and interested. Because the roof joins seamlessly with the surrounding grassland, it is tempting for children to run on to it. 'We have planted a low hedge of *Corokia* and *Coprosma* species at the eastern edge as a barrier to stop them falling off,' says Rhys.

Perhaps the greatest signal of success is the response of a friend on viewing a Google Earth picture of the completed house at the end of the clearly visible driveway: 'It looks as though the house is not built yet!'

THE ROUNDHOUSE

Brithdir Mawr, Wales, United Kingdom • Owner and designer: **Tony Wrench** • Context: **Residential, low-impact building** • Size: **113 m² (1215 sq ft)** • Main purpose of green roof: **Low visual and environmental impact, insulation, wildlife habitat**

THE ROUNDHOUSE is Tony Wrench and Jane Faith's home, situated in a corner of an old field next to a woodland edge and built into a south-facing slope. This wood-framed ecohome is constructed of cobwood walls with recycled windows and a straw-insulated turf roof. The house uses solar power and wind turbine for electricity and has a compost toilet and reed beds for grey water. The Roundhouse embodies Tony Wrench's fundamental beliefs in low-environmental-impact living and building. It was designed and built over the winter of 1997–1998, for a total cost of £3000.

Designing and planning

Tony Wrench designed and planned the green roof himself. He had known about green roofs and liked them for a long time, and he built his first one in 1990. 'I put one on The Roundhouse, because I don't know how to build roofs of any other kind,' says Tony.

Installation

The house is supported and built around sturdy upright timber posts. The roof consists of a cone-shaped structure of 13 main rafters and 100 minor ones. Willow was then woven radially into this framework to form a solid and complete base for the roof. Then canvas (a second-hand marquee) was draped to cover the gaps between the woven willow stems. On top of this, 120 straw bales—tied together in a spiral and with borax sprinkled on it to prevent rotting—were placed as a thick insulation layer. Finally, a large butyl rubber pond liner was fixed over the entire roof to make it waterproof. Finally, 1400 turves (sod) were lifted from a nearby field and laid directly on the pond liner.

Tony had got the house to the stage where the rafters were secure and the radial willow was pinned on, and the straw bales and pond liner ready. Then twenty-five people from our permaculture group came round, and we put on the structure of the roof in a day. Tony then turfed it over the next four weeks with one or two helpers. All the materials were sourced locally except the rubber membrane.

Success of the green roof

Tony says the roof has been a great success. The house is very warm and the roof provides good

The Roundhouse is virtually invisible within its woodland surroundings. Photo by Tony Wrench

insulation. After eight years some small leaks occurred that were caused either by plant roots or by ants. The leaks were easy to locate and mend, but bad news as the straw got wet. They have added a further layer of silage and 1000-gauge black plastic which after four years has not allowed any more leaks. Tony did some rethinking about the water drainage at the edge and installed drainage pipe (8 cm, 3 in) to direct surplus water to one or two places on the eaves.

As well as the turf covering, the roof also supports climbing and scrambling plants rooted at ground level around the building. In keeping with Tony's permaculture ethos, these are productive, fruiting plants. For example, a 'Black Hamburg' grape, together with *Rubus tricolor*, produced 'a kind foot-deep jungle on the south and west sides that produces quite a lot of grapes—14 kilos [30 lb] last year.'

Tony has made several other roundhouses since

this first one, and he has used his experience of living with a green roof to perfect his techniques. He now puts a geotextile such as polyfelt on the straw, then a membrane of two sheets of plastic, then a spiral of drainage pipe, then more polyfelt, then turf. He also uses better fascia boards at the eaves.

As the latest alteration to his own roof, Tony has installed a light box over the bed, which involved cutting a hole down through all the layers in the roof, through which sunlight is magnified into the house. He found about an inch of the top layer of straw had rotted due to condensation (a theoretical problem), but the majority of the straw was still fine. 'I might put a vapour-proof membrane under the straw on the next one I build, to prevent condensation happening at the straw-membrane interface,' says Tony.

GREEN ROOFS
on Bicycle Sheds and Other Small Structures

The completed storage space. Photo by Jonathan Leach

Oxford, United Kingdom • Owner and designer: **Liz Hodgson** • Context: **Bicycle shed in residential front garden** • Size: **1.3 × 2.1 m (4.3 × 7 ft)** • Main purpose of green roof: **Aesthetic, horticulture, stormwater management**

In the summer, gaps fill in with *Dianthus*, annual *Linaria*, and *Sisyrinchium*. Photo by Jonathan Leach

WHILE LIVING in Tours, France, in the 1970s, Liz had seen the Troglodyte houses along the cliffs in the Loire Valley, with chimneys coming up through the grass above. She had also seen a green roof in a front garden on the route to her allotment, and this gave her the idea of trying one of her own.

The bicycle shed is sited along the sidewalk of Liz's small terraced house. It is a very prominent feature in the front garden of the property and quite visible to passers-by. Liz wanted to improve the look of the shed and to create a different growing space for another range of plants in her garden. The green roof was also intended to soak up a little rainwater in a street where front gardens were becoming increasingly paved over, shedding rainwater runoff into a road with inadequate drains.

Designing and planning

Liz had seen a turf roof at the Centre for Alternative Technology at Machynlleth in Wales in 1997 and had been inspired by it. She obtained the plans of the turf roof she had seen at the centre. The dimensions were determined by the existing shed and the materials at hand. Liz chose the plants herself, designing the planting during the execution, not in advance, and then planted new ones that made sense over the next few years.

Far right: The roof is simply constructed over the bicycle shed. Photo by Liz Hodgson

Right: The green roof is very visible to passers-by. In spring, blue grape hyacinths (*Muscari*) are prominent, together with emerging irises, sempervivums, and sedums. Photo by Liz Hodgson

Installation

During a kitchen remodelling in 2006, the builder needed to demolish the bicycle shed temporarily. It was put back retrofitted with the green roof space ready for filling and planting, using leftover materials from the construction.

The builder worked from the Centre for Alternative Technology plans, putting heavy-duty plastic sheeting over the original roof and creating the frame from leftover rafter lengths. The shed had turned out to be very robust and capable of supporting plenty of additional weight. The substrate comprises garden soil left over from reshaping the back garden plus two sacks of John Innes no. 3 (a gritty, free-draining soil-based horticultural compost), with gravel underneath, plus a layer of horticultural grit on top which is renewed periodically.

The plants used were the annual *Linaria maroccana* 'Fairy Bouquet' and the perennials *Achillea millefolium, Anthemis tinctoria, Arenaria balearica, Campanula poscharskyana, Delosperma congestum, Geranium dalmaticum, Helianthemum nummularium* 'Golden Queen', *Phlox douglasii* 'Boothman's Variety', *Saxifraga callosa*, seven *Sedum* cultivars, three *Sempervivum* cultivars including 'Black Knight', and *Sisyrinchium* 'Californian Skies'. Bulbs included four species of *Crocus, Iris reticulata* 'Gordon', *Iris danfordiae, Muscari,* and *Tulipa tarda*. Plants which come in regularly as self-sowers are *Cotoneaster horizontalis, Laburnum*, violets, dandelions, and grasses.

Success of the green roof

Liz didn't anticipate the pleasure the roof would give her, 'The slowing down to look instead of dashing in and out of the house, the fun of watching people inspecting it. Passers-by take photos, hold up little children to look, especially at crocus time, and stop me to say how they love it.'

ever since, and the phlox is named for the nurseryman Stuart Boothman, who taught him about alpines. The grape hyacinths remind me of the big garden at my uncle's farm, where they grew under the old fruit trees. So there's nostalgia and family history all bound up with something quite trendy!'

If Liz were to start again, she might have made the substrate deeper to allow for a wider range of plants, but the challenge of how shallow it is has become part of the fun. It has not experienced a really hot summer yet, so that may not last. She would not have planted *Campanula poscharskyana*, as it is running halfway across the roof already. This species would be ideal for a roof where no varied planting or aftercare is planned or only in combination with bulbs and other rampant plants.

After three and a half years, the green roof is much more of a horticultural success than Liz ever imagined. It's a manageable size, which is great for Liz as she has health issues that prevent her from working on a large scale, and the roof is easily weeded in passing. Although she enjoys rising to the challenge of the shallow substrate and exposed position, problems consist of worrying about whether plants will survive and keeping others under control. Successes are manifold and various, especially over-doing the crocuses, irises, and muscari, with spectacular results. Working out that *Linaria* would thrive and self seed was very satisfying.

The roof reminds Liz of the hours spent with her grandfather in his potting shed fiddling about with alpines and enjoying tiny plants. 'The geranium was rescued from his last garden in 1979 and has survived

NIGEL'S NOTES

Liz nicely describes the everyday delight and fascination that having a green roof can produce. But the project also highlights an important point: not only does a green roof provide benefits to the owner, but it also gives pleasure to others. These may be people living nearby who overlook the roof, or, as in the case of Liz's project, to people who pass by in the street.

Upperthorpe, Sheffield, United Kingdom • Owner and designer: **Dan and Kate Cornwell** • Context: **Garden building and bicycle shed** • Size: **2 m² (22 sq ft)** • Main purpose of green roof: **Aesthetic, horticulture, biodiversity**

The completed shelter. Photo by Dan Cornwell

DAN AND Kate have a very small urban garden in Sheffield and three young children. 'I have a great interest in horticulture, but no space for plants in my garden,' says Dan. The family needed a small storage area in the garden and this seemed a perfect opportunity for a low-maintenance garden that fitted in with their busy lifestyle. With the kitchen window overlooking the roof, this was something they could see up close every day. Dan says, 'It was my chance to have my own two square metres of unspoiled, child-free garden to enjoy.'

Designing and planning

Dan works for Green Estate Ltd. in Sheffield, a social enterprise that works with innovative landscape techniques, and one of their areas of work is as green roof contractors. Dan therefore had access to a lot of knowledge and personal experience of green roof design and installation. He planned and designed the roof himself by looking at other green roof constructions. Dan came up with the final approach through trial and error by testing out different ways of strengthening small garden sheds. He bought an inexpensive timber bicycle shed that could be easily modified, changed the roof from a double to single pitch, and used local inexpensive building materials.

The shed is internally strengthened with batons. Photo by Dan Cornwell

The green roof serves as a small garden right outside the window. Photo by Dan Cornwell

Installation

To alter the pitch and to strengthen the shed, Dan used 100 × 25 mm (4 × 1 in) joists to span the roof at the back and 50 × 25 mm (2 × 1 in) joists at the front. He used 18-mm (0.7-in) external-grade plywood for the roof deck. The interior was reinforced with 30 × 20 mm (1.25 × 0.75 in) batons fitted diagonally across the sides. Plastic sheeting was used for root and waterproofing on to the deck. On this 100 × 20 mm (4 × 0.75 in) boards were used as edges and made a frame to sit on top of the deck. This frame was then screwed from underneath. Inside the frame sat a commercial drainage board (ZinCo FD25) for water retention, with landscape fabric over the top. Green roof substrate was placed at a depth of 100 mm (4 in) and sown with Pictorial Meadows Green Roof seed mix (developed in association with The Green Roof Centre, University of Sheffield) with additional plug planting of herbs and bulbs as a later addition. Subsequently, Dan has added buckets full of substrate turned upside down on the roof to sow new plants into and create more diversity as required.

Success of the green roof

The roof is low maintenance. Dan says, 'I really enjoy seeing the planting change through the seasons and watching the birds and insects visiting the flowers as I do the washing up. It was well worth the effort considering the enjoyment we get from it.' Spring bulbs such as dwarf narcissus give a real seasonal highlight, and the family grow culinary herbs such as thyme, coriander, chives, and parsley. 'The planting is quite diverse on the roof and very wild looking, which I really like,' says Dan, 'but Kate thinks it is quite scruffy and should be tidied up with more flowers.'

London, United Kingdom • Owner and designer: **Joe Swift** • Context: **Bicycle shelter** • Size: **4 × 1.2 m (13 × 4 ft)** • Main purpose of green roof: **Aesthetic, horticulture, biodiversity**

The completed storage space. Photo by Joe Swift

JOE WANTED to have somewhere to keep his family's bicycles, but space was very limited in his London front garden, with only a few metres from the front door of the house to the sidewalk and road. There was no room to put in any major structures. As a garden designer and a presenter of the United Kingdom's main gardening television programme, Joe had a good amount of knowledge and experience of green roofs and was very enthusiastic about innovative ways to incorporate biodiversity into the built structures of a garden.

Designing and planning

Outhouses, structures, and buildings in front of the house usually require planning permission in the United Kingdom. Joe's solution was to conceal the bicycles from the street and to have them securely fixed by incorporating a lock-up area within a new wall along the front edge of the garden alongside the street. The wall was built in the traditional style, and it looks no different from any other townhouse front garden wall.

Installation

The area below where the bicycles would be was dug out to increase the depth available for the bicycles. Drainage was incorporated to allow water to runoff. The wall was built up, and as the roof deck purpose-fabricated galvanized metal trays were fixed into the wall, with a supporting middle leg. Drainage holes

From the front, the bicycle shelter is invisible. Photo by Joe Swift

were drilled into the trays, and a lightweight polystyrene sheet was put in the base for drainage. The trays were then backfilled with regular horticultural compost, with added perlite to increase drainage.

Success of the green roof

Foxes immediately started digging up the trays every night, so Joe had to put some chicken wire over the top of the compost to put a stop to it. The bicycle shelter is in a shady, north-facing position and hardly gets any sun. Joe says, 'I'm just seeing what turns up and leaving bits in that can cope so it fills out well.' He sowed some shady wildflower seed, and he planted in some garden cast-offs such as *Salvia nemerosa* 'Ostrfriesland' and some pinks (*Dianthus*). He also I put in some sunflowers, which did flower even though the site is shady. 'The red campion (*Silene dioica*) has gone a bit mad, but after flowering I'll thin it out,' says Joe. He also put in some annual and biennial seeds (cornflowers and verbascums) and will plant some bulbs in the autumn. The roof does get dry, so Joe waters it occasionally if things look desperate.

NIGEL'S NOTES

Joe's structure is a very simple and clever low-tech solution for hiding away a storage area in a small space. The idea of setting a green roof into a boundary wall in this way can be modified and adapted using a wide range of materials.

COMMUNITY PROJECTS

The wildflowers and grasses on this green roof complement the meadow on the ground.
Photo by John Little

CLAPTON PARK
COMMUNITY GARDEN SHELTER

Hackney, London, United Kingdom • Owner: **Clapton Park Management Organising** • Designer: **John Little** • Context: **Public, community garden** • Size: **2.4 × 3.5 m (8 × 11.5 ft)** • Main purpose of green roof: **Biodiversity, aesthetic**

The shelter in the community garden. Photo by Jane Sebire

In 1994 the residents of Clapton Park housing estate, Hackney, London, took advantage of a new government initiative and voted to opt out of council control. The residents would be in charge and make the decisions about their own estate, and a decision-making board of local residents was formed. In 2002 they turned their attention to the green space around the estate and in particular the grounds maintenance. They invited three new companies to tender, one of which was the Grass Roof Company. During the pitch for the contract, John Little mused about flower edges, food growing, and, of course, green roofs. The board decided to take a chance, and the Grass Roof Company were appointed, despite having no track record in grounds maintenance.

The aesthetic advantages of living roofs were recognized early by the board. Like most other inner-city estates, Clapton Park was dominated by three- and four-storey buildings. Most of the residents therefore looked down on roofs—boring roofs.

In 2004, when the residents won some funding to improve one of the community gardens, John finally got his chance to build the estate's first green roof on a new shelter in the garden. The garden was also to include naturalistic planting based on work pioneered in Sheffield, oak raised beds to give space for residents to plant in, wildflower meadows, and a small copse of native trees, all given a contrasting formal edge of paths and lawn. Three floors of the adjacent block surrounded and overlooked the new garden.

Designing and planning

The new shelter was designed to be open-sided with simple diagonal bracing to ensure the rigidity needed for the top-heavy structure. The residents also wanted to be sure there were 'no places to hide,' and John wanted the building to be dominated by plants, so the open sides made sense for several reasons. The timber floor was built flush with the paths to give good wheelchair access, and the budget was stretched to include lighting to extend its use into the evenings. The whole building cost £3000 in 2004.

Installation

Timber beams were fixed with large galvanized bolts to the timber uprights, and joists were fixed on top of these to form the two-level roof. The whole roof was waterproofed with a 1-mm (0.04-in) butyl rubber liner, and felt was laid on top to protect the liner. Then the roof was filled with soil and brick rubble from the foundations. (This rubble is from previous dwellings demolished after the war.) The mix of soil and rubble proved to be important in providing extra drainage and in relieving the anaerobic conditions that are often a problem in a flat green roof. The plants were brought down to the roof edge by not using a fascia and allowing the water to drip off the front edge. The soil and plants were trapped using some of the felt, and this was laid under the substrate, up, and back on itself. Holes were then cut in the felt and plants pushed through into the soil. A drip was formed along this edge to allow the water to drip away from the structure. No irrigation system was installed on the roof.

The Grass Roof Company were keen to explore planting options other than the formulaic sedum blankets. The estate was becoming known for its biodiversity-friendly landscapes, and in particular the colourful annuals that lined the railings of the

GRASSES ▶
AND
HERBACEOUS
PLANTS

geotextile ▶
geotextile ▶

LINER
ROOF DECK

The green roof build-up. Drawing by Evangelia Bakratsa

estate. The board thought it would be good to add a few poppies (*Papaver rhoeas*) and corn chamomile (*Anthemis arvensis*) to the mix, even though these plants would probably only persist for the first couple of years. Perennials were mixed with the wild cards provided by the residents. John says, 'The Hottentot fig (*Carpobrotus chilensis*) donated by one of the ladies on the ground floor is still growing well, and we now use this species on a lot of our roofs.' Other plants donated included *Sedum reflexum*. John also added natives such as wild sorrel (*Rumex acetosa*), lady's bedstraw (*Galium verum*), viper's bugloss (*Echium vulgare*), yarrow (*Achillea millefolium*), thrift (*Armeria maritima*), ox-eye daisy (*Leucanthemum vulgare*) and non-natives such as *Stipa* and *Dianthus*.

Success of the green roof

Plenty of rain fell in London during the first year, so the annuals made a good show and the rest of the planting established well. Two drought years followed, and many of the original species died off in the relatively shallow 100-mm (4-in) substrate. This tended to open up the vegetation and allow some wind-blown and dormant seed in the original substrate to germinate and take over some of the roof. This has meant the roof has a much grassier and unkempt look, something the contractors and board are hoping the residents will not be too concerned about.

The board is very keen not to lose public support for green roofs as they have plans to green up thirty-two garages in another part of the estate. John says, 'I think we may have to spend some time on this roof to bring back some of the more traditional garden feel that the residents enjoyed at the start.' They plan to retrofit by adding areas of deeper substrate and removing some of the less-attractive species that have invaded the space. Other more reliable green roof plants could then be added.

The roof, even with its more unkempt look, still complements the garden's natural feel. Residents living opposite the garden say, 'People are always asking why there are plants on the garden roof. We are still not sure but we like it anyway.'

JOHN'S NOTES

I think this roof should have more of a garden-border feel. We plan to replant and add more substrate to achieve this. I am keen to keep the residents on our side by going against my usual preference for native and diverse roofs and managing this one purely for aesthetics.

HERRINGHAM PRIMARY SCHOOL OUTDOOR CLASSROOM

Chadwell St Mary, Essex, United Kingdom • Owner: **Herringham Primary School** • Green roof consultant: **John Little** • Context: **School** • Size: **22 m² (237 sq ft)** • Main purpose of green roof: **Biodiversity, aesthetic**

IN 2005 Mary McKinnon oversaw the amalgamation of the infant and junior schools into Herringham Primary School. She was keen to transform the outdoor space around her new school into a place the kids would want to use. Mary especially liked the idea of an outdoor classroom complete with living roof and teacher's chair. Back in 2000 she had worked with John Little of the Grass Roof Company, and she decided to meet with him and other teachers to start a design. The building would be a focal point for environmental learning and provide space for art and design to be displayed. Being accessible to waiting parents, it would be a great place to show off some of the kids' work. The friends and parents of Herringham School started work raising money for the project. By 2007 sufficient funds had been raised, work began on the classroom in July 2008.

Designing and planning

Mary wanted some permanent shade and somewhere a class of children could come and learn all year round. The site chosen was a well-worn piece of grass surrounded by fruit and birch trees. The design was to fit into the arc formed by the trees and was to have a sense of fun and ecology, a mix not often seen together. A combination of Forest Stewardship Council–certified timber, recycled plastic, and reclaimed timber was used to build a fan-shaped building capable of seating around thirty kids. The entire structure was lifted up from the ground using small concrete supports, lead moisture-proofing, and stainless steel locating pins. This meant the structure would 'last as long as the school,' as Mary had insisted.

The Grass Roof Company had always looked to try various recycled and reclaimed materials as growing medium, but after eight years thought they should try one of the many proprietary substrates that were available. They also decided to increase the depth in places up to around 200 mm (8 in) to give a wider range of plants a chance to survive even without irrigation. This meant a weight loading of 230 kg/m² (47 lb/sq ft), around 4 tons across the whole roof.

Installation

Most of the walls of the classroom were lined with 18-mm (0.7-in) plywood. This, combined with the building's fan shape, gave the very rigid wall section

Left: A miniature green roof at children's level shows what is on the classroom roof. Photo by John Little

Below left: The outdoor classroom, with teacher's chair. Photo by John Little

Below: Mounding the substrate, with an irrigation line beneath. Photo by John Little

Logs, bricks, stones, old rope, and mounded substrate increases the biodiversity value of the roof. Photo by John Little

the contractors needed to allow this greater depth of growing medium. The design also ensured a short roof span, so the 200-mm (8-in) substrate depth was easy to support without the need for any more than 150 × 50 mm (6 × 2 in) joists. The open front of the building was supported on double 200 × 50 mm (8 × 2 in) beams fixed on each side of 90-mm (3.5-in) square posts with 16-mm-diameter (0.6-in) galvanized bolts. The contractors' preferred choice of butyl rubber was used to waterproof the structure. The flexibility and long life of this material was felt to outweigh the extra care needed during installation. Butyl rubber is less puncture-resistant than some of the other proprietary products, but once installed correctly will give a virtually life-long seal.

The standard 100-mm (4-in) edge around the roof was used, and the extra depth of material was simply mounded back from the roof edge. This meant the roof structure did not look too heavy and the plants would be more visible despite the flat roof design.

In the end the Grass Roof team could not bring themselves to order all the substrate from a commercial source, so instead they split the 4 tons of material between the proprietary brand and the crushed ceramic waste (crushed basins) they had used on a recent project. They laid the more freely draining ceramics as a base beneath the more moisture retentive commercial material. No drainage mat was used, and instead the substrate was shaped to form mounds and troughs that directed the excess water back to the two drainage outlets. Irrigation was also installed— it was felt that at this stage it makes sense even if it's only used to establish the newly planted roof.

As the school children had been involved during most of the design and construction, a note was sent home with the kids to ask for drought-tolerant plants or any suitable waste materials they thought could be used on the roof. The contractors combined these with some waste from the project and car tyres to create the diversity of materials and plants that

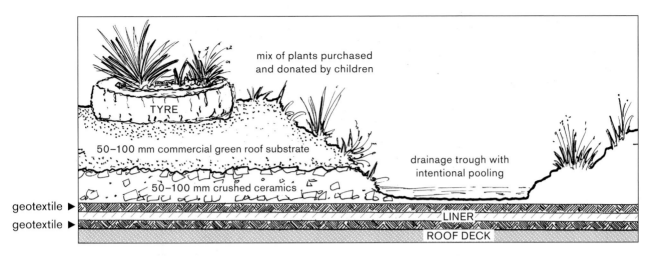

The green roof build-up. Drawing by Evangelia Bakratsa

had now become the Grass Roof Company's trademark. The planting was finished off with Hottentot fig (*Carpobrotus chilensis*) for the roof edge, a couple of taller *Miscanthus* grasses, and a green roof seed mix developed by Nigel Dunnett from Sheffield University. The total cost of the building with roof was £6900 in 2008.

There was a thriving gardening club at the school run by a very enthusiastic teacher, so during the construction it was suggested a miniature green roof could be built at kids' level. This would provide the gardening club a new addition to their green space and give an indication at ground level what was going on above.

Success of the green roof

The extra substrate depth has meant the larger specimen plants are thriving, and there is a good mix of plants on the different soil depths created by the mounding and hollows. The ceramics seem to be allowing the water to drain sufficiently, and the deliberate pooling designed into one corner of the roof is providing a high-level bird bath. A rooftop web cam has also been suggested, and the Grass Roof Company are currently trying to arrange for a regular invertebrate survey. Monitoring of small-scale green roof fauna has been very poor, so it's increasingly important that these roofs start to give back information to influence future design.

Before work had started on the classroom, the contractors were approached by a television company to feature one of their green-roofed buildings. John Little had always had a soft spot for the school and thought it would be great to get the film crew to see it. The kids from the gardening club came out and filled their miniature roof with substrate while the contractors completed the main roof. The kids were great, and the programme aired in September of that year.

LINCEWOOD PRIMARY SCHOOL OUTDOOR CLASSROOM

Langdon Hills, Basildon, Essex, United Kingdom • Owner: **Lincewood School** • Designer: **John Little** • Context: **School** • Size: **5 × 5 m (16.5 × 16.5 ft)** • Main purpose of green roof: **Biodiversity, wildlife habitat, education**

LINCEWOOD SCHOOL is tucked away against the edge of an Essex Wildlife Trust reserve on the side of Langdon Hills. The outdoor classroom is located in a quiet area in the far corner of the grounds, next to some of the beautiful oak woodland of the reserve. The space had a scattering of picnic benches on a bark floor, and from here old grassland slopes steeply up to the school boundary and woods beyond. The school, and in particular Sarah Smith, chair of the Parent-Teachers Association, were keen for this backdrop of classic English countryside to be linked to the design for a new outdoor classroom.

On one of the school's regular visits to the local wildlife trust reserve, Sarah saw a new living roof shelter built for the park, using all reclaimed and recycled materials. She knew this was exactly the feel she wanted for the classroom, and reserve staff put her in touch with the Grass Roof Company. Lincewood School liked the look of an outdoor classroom they had just built for another local school. A meeting was arranged with John Little, partner in the company, and the details of the design were thrashed out.

Designing and planning

The school knew that they wanted the building to do more than just shelter the children, so a wish list was compiled. Building materials were to be Forest Stewardship Council–certified, reclaimed, recycled, or locally sourced. The structure had to create shade and seat thirty children. The whole building should become a habitat in its own right. The roof was to be alive, designed to encourage biodiversity, and have some link to the surrounding space. Finally, the Grass Roof Company would follow the construction with a school assembly where John could enthuse and inform the kids about their new classroom, as well as provide a twice yearly maintenance programme.

A major feature of the design was the cladding. The outside of the building was clad with oak and ash planking, the edges of which would remain naturally irregular. A couple of months before the work started in March 2008, John met with volunteers from the country park who were keen to cut the planking from logs from the park. When fixed to the outside of the timber frame, gaps allowed for birds and other wildlife to make use of the wall

The green roof is a great educational resource and blends well with the building's surroundings. Photo by John Little

cavity to nest and hibernate. Sheep's wool and other nesting material was also added to the cavity before the strand board sheets were fixed on the inside wall to enclose the space. This meant that the walls would become the habitat the kids had wanted. Recycled plastic and reclaimed cedar was used to trim the windows and roof edge.

Installation

The roof was supported by three sets of double 200 × 50 mm (8 × 2 in) beams onto which 150 × 50 mm (6 × 2 in) joists were fixed. There was no attempt to slope the roof, as a small amount of pooling would add to the mix of growing conditions on the roof. A 1-mm (0.04-in) butyl rubber liner from a local supplier, complete with outlet, was used to waterproof the roof. The liner was protected top and bottom with a geotextile felt from the same source.

As a substrate, 3 tons of crushed ceramics made from old sinks, basins, and toilets was put up in a ratio 9:1 of ceramics to green waste compost. To increase the biodiversity potential further, the growing medium was sculpted to vary the depth from 10 mm (0.5 in) where the water laid up to 250 mm (10 in) above the main roof supports. Other physical elements, including old tyres and logs from the woodland, were also added before the roof was planted. This gave a variety of conditions to suit a wide range of plant and invertebrate species.

The contractors looked at the grass bank surrounding the building and found several plant species that were worth trying on the new roof. So native species typical of calcareous or chalk grasslands, such as bird's foot trefoil (*Lotus corniculatus*), selfheal (*Prunella vulgaris*), hawkbit (*Leontodon hispidus*), and grasses including crested dogs

The green roof sits in a quiet area on the edge of the school
grounds, next to oak woodland. Photo by John Little

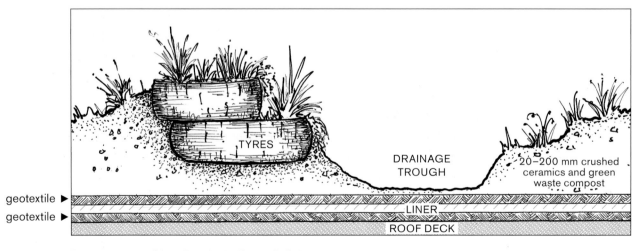

The green roof build-up. Drawing by Evangelia Bakratsa

tail (*Cynosurus cristatus*) were duly ordered from Landlife Wild Flowers, ready to add to the classic green roof species used previously. A green roof seed mix developed by Nigel Dunnett and sold through Green Estate Ltd. complemented the mix of plug plants. The total cost of the building was £6900 in 2008.

Success of the green roof

The weather conditions proved ideal for establishing the planting, and a return visit from the contractors four months later revealed more than twenty-five species already growing well. The ceramics and green waste compost proved to be very weed free, so the only maintenance necessary in the first year was to remove a few wind-blown seedlings. No irrigation was installed, and it is not expected that the roof will ever be watered; it will be interesting to see what plants survive long-term under this combination of conditions. The Grass Roof Company are keen to monitor the changes in the roof and have agreed to inspect the roof over the coming years, including a plant and invertebrate survey. John has suggested that during each visit photos of the roof be taken and sent to the school along with details of the changes.

The school's head teacher and Sarah both say the new classroom has given them a place to focus on environmental issues in the school. It's good to have a practical example of a green building and recycled materials on site. The roof blends into the grass bank and has provoked interest and discussion from the parents, teachers, and children.

The roof has a varied topography, and old logs add to the wildlife value. Photo by John Little

JOHN'S NOTES

This is one of my favourite roofs. By using small plug plant and seeds, the plants have grown up with the substrate and the water stress. This, combined with the relatively low nutrient levels, meant the plants grew slowly so when the first drought of the summer came they were able to cope. The mix of substrate depths and materials like tyres, logs, and rubble has now become an essential on our roofs. They give the variation of microhabitats that really make green roofs work.

The bike shelter. Photo by Jane Sebire

The Grass Roof Company had always insisted a separate drainage layer was not generally necessary, and with free-draining pumice as a substrate this roof would definitely not need one. Pumice, although light and effective, has lots of embedded energy (that is, the total energy required in producing and transporting a product) because of the long-distance transport required and was perhaps not the most sustainable choice, but at the time the alternatives were not so well understood. A sedum blanket was chosen to cover the pumice. This would give an instant impact for the visitors, and the sedums, although not all natives, were not expected to colonize the clay soil of the surrounding reserve.

The roof of the wood shed, however, was to have the relatively fertile soil dug from the footings as the growing medium. Sarah thought it would be good to have this contrast of the stressed dry roof on the bicycle shelter and the lush grassy roof above the wood shed. More care would have to be taken with the plant mix for this roof, so a turf of native grasses and wildflowers was ordered from a local supplier.

Flower species included lesser knapweed (*Centaurea nigra*), wild sorrel (*Rumex acetosa*), bird's foot trefoil (*Lotus corniculatus*), and yarrow (*Achillea millefolium*). The grasses were dominated by the drought-resistant crested fox tail (*Cynosurus cristatus*). Unfortunately, the wood shed could only be 3.6 × 2.4 m (12 × 8 ft), which meant the building took on the top-heavy appearance difficult to avoid when greening a small structure.

Both buildings and the wildlife garden were finished by the end of 2004. The cost of the bicycle shelter was £4900, and the cost to construct the wood shed was £3200.

Success of the green roofs

The bicycle shelter and roof have been successful in giving visitors an intimate small-scale example of sustainable construction and living roofs within a wildlife trust reserve. Sarah has left, but the visitor centre's education officer says the public are intrigued by the roofs and this interest often leads on to discussion about the trust's work on reducing its energy use. They hope to provide more interpretation within the bicycle shelter on these issues, in the hope that visitors take away an interest in green building as well as the core wildlife conservation message.

Ironically, the bicycle shelter has not been successful in attracting bicycles. Many visitors come on bicycles, but they tend to continue on around the reserve rather than lock them up and explore by foot. There are plans to use some of the space within

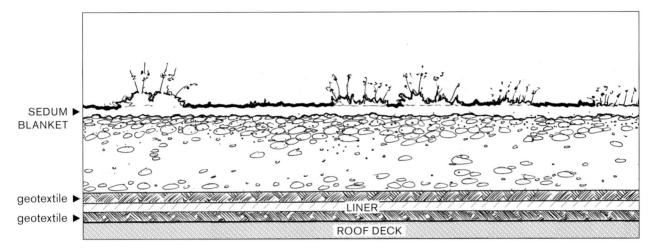

SEDUM BLANKET ▶

geotextile ▶

geotextile ▶

LINER

ROOF DECK

The build-up of the bicycle shelter green roof. Drawing by Evangelia Bakratsa

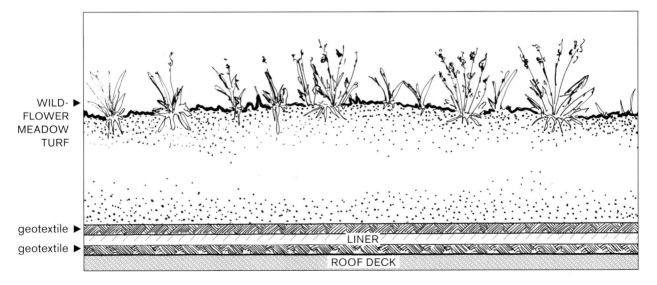

WILD-FLOWER MEADOW TURF ▶

geotextile ▶

geotextile ▶

LINER

ROOF DECK

The build-up of the wood shed green roof. Drawing by Evangelia Bakratsa

Sedum album flowering on the bicycle shelter roof. Photo by John Little

the shelter for interpretation about the history of the plotlands and the people who lived there.

Neither roof has ever been irrigated, and John is pleased that both still support much of the original planting. The sedum roof is obviously stressed from the nutrient loss over the past seven years, but it remains relatively varied. Surprisingly, the only other plants that have managed to colonize the sedum are grasses, mainly crested fox tail from the adjacent wood shed roof. John suggested the trust and volunteers could grow some plants from seed collected on the reserve. Plants found growing in the rubble from the ruins of the old plotland houses would be a great source as they would be capable of coping with the similar conditions found on the roof. Green roof substrate could be used to grow these on until they were ready to be planted out. More of this substrate would be mounded into gaps

in the sedum to help establish the new introductions. John feels this retrofitting of existing green roofs would make real sense: 'It will allow us to apply our knowledge gained over the past ten years to some of the less inspiring early sedum roofs.'

The wood shed roof is also less vigorous now but continues to support a similar number of species as in the original mix. Some species that could not cope with the anaerobic conditions of the early winters have gone or just managed to hang on along the top ridge. On the other hand, sedums such as *Sedum reflexum* are starting to colonize the gravel drainage gulley at the base of the roof.

Staff look on their green-roofed buildings with some affection. They describe thinking of them as being alive, which, after all, is what wildlife conservation should be about.

JOHN'S NOTES

I like the idea of retrofitting some of the early sedum roofs. Extra weight loading may be an issue, but this could be overcome by adding the extra substrate over the building supports. The soggy conditions associated with green roofs filled with normal soil from the site do improve once a fibrous root system is established and can also be offset by forming mounds and gullies.

ONE TREE HILL SHELTER

Langdon Hills Country Park, Thurrock, Essex, United Kingdom • Owner: Thurrock Council • Designer: **John Little** • Context: **Public community building** • Size: **18 m² (195 sq ft) and 10 m² (108 sq ft)** • Main purpose of green roof: **Biodiversity, aesthetic**

The building houses recycling facilities, and the wall panels contain examples of the items that can be recycled there. Photo by John Little

NICK STANLEY is senior ranger for the Langdon Hills country park in Thurrock, Essex. In 2005 he was looking to replace an existing notice board with a much more ambitious structure to both give space for interpretation and shelter for school groups and visitors to the park. Nick hoped to encourage more recycling and to extend the park's remit by promoting the use of sustainable and local materials within buildings. He also, of course, wanted to add to the biodiversity in the park. He hoped a living roof would help the building merge into the hill behind and most importantly reflect the council and park's commitment to green buildings. Nick had seen the work that local contractor John Little from the Grass Roof Company had been doing in the schools around the park and asked him to come up with a scheme.

Designing and planning

John wanted to design a practical space for the public to shelter from the sun and rain, but just as

importantly, they wanted it to be a wildlife habitat and as sustainable as possible in its construction.

The building has two separate roofs. One slopes in one direction (monopitch) and uses reclaimed soil and green waste compost, and the other is flat and filled with crushed brick and concrete. The intention for the contrasting substrates was that the soil would encourage relatively dense rank growth on the monopitch and a more sparse diverse community on the rubble roof. Both roofs are planted with drought-tolerant species but also with bare space between to encourage the soil and concrete to heat up, which is important for invertebrates.

Installation

The walls of the building are thin panels filled with log sections from the park, crushed concrete, cans, and bottles. In effect they are like very thin gabion structures, with steel mesh retaining the contents. Gaps are left between the cladding to provide space for birds to nest in the wall cavity, as well as lengths of bamboo cane mixed in with the log wall for solitary bees and lacewings.

Nick and the volunteers from the park collected planking from various tree species, and log sections were cut to 100 mm (4 in) to fit into the wall cavities. Aluminium cans from the recycling bins in the park

Far left: The roof soon after planting. Photo by John Little

Above: Once established, the two roofs developed different vegetation depending on the substrate. Photo by John Little

Left: Thin log sections in the panels provide invertebrate habitat. Photo by Nigel Dunnett

were chosen for their different colours and brands. 'Most difficult of all was the work that went into supplying several hundred stubby bottles of Stella Artois lager to create the bottle wall. In the end it took three months of drinking to get the total needed,' says John.

The structural upright timbers of the building are made from a reclaimed tropical hardwood called Ekki, cut from old railway sleepers. The roof beams were made from Greenheart, another reclaimed tropical hardwood. The roof joists were reclaimed soft wood painted with organic paint, and the facia and roof trim were reclaimed western red cedar, locally sourced. The roof deck comprised Forest Stewardship Council–certified 18-mm (0.7 in) plywood. The cladding and benches were built from timber taken from the park. The whole building sat on individual pad footings to further limit the embedded energy of the structure.

By using reclaimed tropical hardwoods for the main structure of the roof, the dimensions of the beam were much smaller than would have been the case with the equivalent softwood. The huge strength of Greenheart and Ekki beams meant the construction dimensions looked similar to a roof with only conventional weight loading. The joist ends were also chamfered down to 50 mm (2 in) to further lighten the look of the roof. The fascia depth was kept to a minimum. Both roofs were waterproofed using a 1-mm (0.04 in) butyl rubber liner. This was protected by layers of geotextile top and bottom, but the top layer had to be particularly tough to prevent the crushed brick and concrete from damaging the liner.

A 7:3 ratio of crushed brick to concrete varying

Roofs with lower fertility substrate that vary in depth are important in delivering the mix of flora and fauna that really add to the local biodiversity.

Wall panels. Photo by Nigel Dunnett

from 100 to 150 mm (4–6 in) deep was put up on to the flat roof. The monopitch roof was filled with soil from the building footings mixed with green waste compost from the local recycling plant to a depth of 100–150 mm (4–6 in). Because of the short fascia, the substrate was mounded up from the roof edge to get the desired depth. Using plugs and seed, a mix of drought-resistant species were planted, including the perennials viper's bugloss (*Echium vulgare*), thyme (*Thymus vulgaris*), small scabious (*Scabiosa columbaria*), *Sedum album*, thrift (*Armeria maritima*), chives (*Allium schoenoprasum*), prostrate rosemary (*Rosmarinus officinalis* 'Prostratus'), and quaking grass (*Briza media*) and the annuals field poppy (*Papaver rhoeas*), corn flower (*Centaurea cyanus*), and corn chamomile (*Anthemis arvensis*).

The cost of the project was £6900 in 2008, including the building and landscaping.

Success of the green roof

The roof with the rich soil and compost was quickly dominated by rank grasses and weeds, especially over the two wet summers of 2008 and 2009. Nick is hopeful that some of these will die out in subsequent years during the drought periods now common in southeastern England. The crushed brick and rubble roof supports a more interesting and diverse flora, although even this roof is suffering from poor drainage associated with the high brick content of the roof substrate. Nick and John have plans to remedy the drainage problem by mounding the substrate to create gulleys that lead back to the outlet, which will also add to the microhabitats on the roof. The overlap created by the two roofs has produced a drier

The rain chain directs runoff water to ground level. Photo by John Little

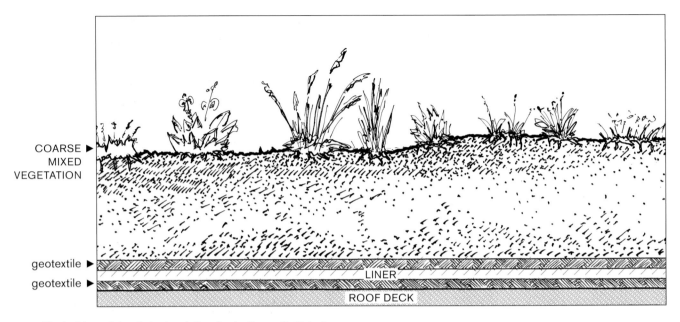

COARSE
MIXED
VEGETATION ▶

geotextile ▶

LINER

geotextile ▶

ROOF DECK

The build-up of the pitched roof. Drawing by Evangelia Bakratsa

NATIVE ▶
PLANTS
AND
GRASSES

RUBBLE PILE

geotextile ▶

LINER

geotextile ▶

ROOF DECK

The build-up of the sloped roof. Drawing by Evangelia Bakratsa

zone beneath that is now dominated by sedums, which struggle to compete with the grasses and more vigorous flora that have come to dominate the wetter areas. On the positive side, Nick recommends red valerian (*Centranthus ruber*) for good colour, prostrate rosemary for the roof edge, and viper's bugloss for its ability to seed around.

The building and roof have provoked debate both constructive, inane, and in some cases quite bizarre. Visitors are both amused and bewildered, but Nick says, 'Any response is better than none at all. At least they notice the space now.' He adds, 'We recently noticed the outline of two people in the grass on the roof. We are counting these sunbathers as additions to our biodiversity count for the roof!' Nick is keen to have a formal roof survey, 'It makes sense to gather statistics from the roof in the same way we collect data from the park. The roof gives us a very dry habitat that contrasts to the bulk of the park.'

At the moment the water from the roof is discharged onto a set of galvanized chains clumped under the outlet. Nick is keen to make more use of the water and hopes to release the runoff into a small pond or to direct it back onto the walls of the building to irrigate some planting he is trying to establish in the wall space. He also wants to add to the habitats within the building by incorporating bumble

bee and bug boxes. Other suggestions include integral bird boxes with Perspex backs to allow viewing from inside the shelter. Nick feels that, regardless of the perceived success of the roof in terms of species variety, it has great benefit in that it always promotes debate and reinforces the council's and park's commitment to wider environmental issues.

JOHN'S NOTES

The two separate roofs were important in giving variation in substrate and pitch on one building. In subsequent years they proved to be a textbook example of the resulting contrast in flora with different types of substrate. The lack of plant diversity on the fertile sloping roof has reinforced what I think we already knew: roofs with lower fertility substrate that vary in depth are important in delivering the mix of flora and fauna that really add to the local biodiversity.

PLANT DIRECTORY

Plants with a positive substrate depth (+) require at least 10 cm (4 in) of substrate, whereas those with a negative value (−) can tolerate depths below 10 cm (4 in).

PLANT	COMMON NAME	TYPE	SUBSTRATE DEPTH
Achillea millefolium	yarrow	perennial	+
Allium schoenoprasum	chives	bulb	−
Alyssum maritimum	sweet alyssum	annual	−
Anthoxanthum odoratum	sweet vernal grass	grass	−
Armeria maritima	sea thrift	perennial	−
Briza media	quaking grass	grass	−
Buphthalmum salicifolium	yellow ox-eye	perennial	+
Calamintha nepeta	catmint	perennial	+
Campanula glomerata	clustered bellflower	perennial	+
Campanula rotundifolia	harebell	perennial	−
Centaurea scabiosa	greater knapweed	perennial	+
Clinopodium vulgare	wild basil	perennial	−
Coreopsis tinctoria	tickseed	annual	+
Delosperma cooperi		perennial, succulent	−
Dianthus carthusianorum		perennial	−
Dianthus deltoides	maiden pink	perennial	−
Echium vulgare	viper's bugloss	perennial	−
Euphorbia cyparissias	cypress spurge	perennial	−
Galium verum	lady's bedstraw	perennial	−
Hieracium pilosella	hawkbit	perennial	−
Koeleria glauca		grass	−
Koeleria macrantha		grass	−
Lavandula angustifolia	lavender	perennial	+
Leontodon autumnalis	autumn hawkbit	perennial	−

PLANT	COMMON NAME	TYPE	SUBSTRATE DEPTH
Linaria maroccana	fairy toadflax	annual	−
Lotus corniculatus	birds foot trefoil	perennial	−
Origanum vulgare	oregano	perennial	+
Orostachys boehmeri		succulent	−
Papaver rhoeas	field poppy	annual	+
Petrorhagia saxifraga	tunic plant	perennial	−
Primula veris	cowslip	perennial	−
Prunella vulgaris	selfheal	perennial	−
Pulsatilla vulgaris	pasque flower	perennial	+
Saponaria ocymoides	soapwort	perennial	−
Sedum acre	biting stonecrop	perennial, succulent	−
Sedum album	white stonecrop	perennial, succulent	−
Sedum floriferum 'Weihenstephaner Gold'		perennial	−
Sedum hybridum 'Immergrünchen'		perennial	−
Sedum kamtschaticum		perennial, succulent	−
Sedum reflexum		perennial	−
Sedum rupestre		perennial, succulent	−
Sedum sexangulare		perennial	−
Sedum spurium		perennial	−
Talinum calycinum	flameflower	perennial	−
Teucrium chamaedrys	wall germander	perennial	−
Thymus pulegioides	thyme	perennial	−
Thymus serphyllum	thyme	perennial	−

RESOURCES

Websites

Because the green roof world develops rapidly, the best sources of information are the major green roof websites. The sites listed here not only provide a comprehensive overview of the properties and benefits of green roofs, they also contain an unrivalled resource of inspirational projects. Moreover, they are an excellent source of contacts for local and regional suppliers.

www.greenroofs.org
www.greenroofs.com
www.thegreenroofcentre.co.uk
www.livingroofs.org
greenroofs.wordpress.com

Selected International Green Roof Companies

These companies supply all the main green roof components for large-scale domestic or residential projects but are unlikely to work on very small projects.

American Hydrotech, Inc.
303 East Ohio Street
Chicago, Illinois 60611-3387
United States
Phone: +1 800 877 6125
Fax: +1 312 661 0731
www.hydrotechusa.com

Roofscapes, Inc.
7135 Germantown Avenue, 2nd Floor
Philadelphia, Pennsylvania 19119-1842
United States
Phone: +1 215 247 8784
Fax: +1 215 247 4659
E-mail: info@roofmeadow.com
www.roofmeadow.com

Erisco-Bauder Ltd.
Broughton House
Broughton Road
Ipswich
Suffolk IP1 3QR
United Kingdom
Phone: +44 01473 257 671
Fax: +44 01473 230 761
E-mail: systems@erisco-bauder.co.uk
www.erisco-bauder.co.uk

ZinCo GmbH
Grabenstrasse 33
D-72669 Unterensingen
Germany
Phone: +49 7022 6003 0
Fax: +49 7022 6003 300
E-mail: info@zinco-greenroof.com
www.zinco-greenroof.com

Optigrün International AG
Am Birkenstock 19
D-72505 Krauchenwies-Göggingen
Germany
Phone: +49 0 7576 772 0
Fax: +49 0 7576 772 299
E-mail: info@optigruen.de
www.optigruen.de

Green Roof Suppliers

The following suppliers provide the materials and components for small-scale green roofs and may also offer a contracting service.

Emory Knoll Farms, Inc. (green roof plant suppliers)
3410 Ady Rd.
Street, Maryland 21154
United States
Phone: +1 410 452 5880
Fax: +1 410 452 5319
www.greenroofplants.com

Living Roofs, Inc.
24 Unadilla Alley
Asheville, North Carolina 28803
United States
Phone: +1 828 252 4449
E-mail: info@livingroofsinc.com
www.livingroofsinc.com

The Grass Roof Company
Hilldrop
Laindon Road
Horndon on the Hill SS17 8QB
United Kingdom
Phone: +44 01375 643 576
E-mail: enquiries@grassroofcompany.co.uk
www.grassroofcompany.co.uk

Green Estate Ltd.
Manor Oaks Farmhouse
389 Manor Lane
Sheffield S2 1UL
United Kingdom
Phone: +44 01142 762 828
Fax: +44 01142 677 636

E-mail: info@greenestate.org
www.greenestate.org.uk

Blackdown Horticultural Consultants Ltd.
Combe St. Nicholas
Chard
Somerset TA20 3HZ
United Kingdom
Phone: +44 01460 234 582
www.greenroof.co.uk

Lindum (suppliers of pregrown green roof vegetation)
West Grange
Thorganby
York YO19 6DJ

United Kingdom
Phone: +44 01904 448 675
Fax: +44 01904 448 713
E-mail: lindum@turf.co.uk
www.turf.co.uk

Pictorial Meadows (suppliers of green roof seed mix)
Manor Oaks Farmhouse
389 Manor Lane
Sheffield S2 1UL
United Kingdom
Phone: +44 01142 677 635
Fax: +44 01142 677 636
Email: info@greenestate.org
www.pictorialmeadows.co.uk

BIBLIOGRAPHY

Cantor, Steven L. 2008. *Green Roofs in Sustainable Landscape Design.* W.W. Norton & Co., New York.

Dunnett, Nigel, and Andy Clayden. 2007. *Rain Gardens: Managing Water Sustainability in the Garden and Designed Landscape.* Timber Press, Portland, Oregon.

Dunnett, Nigel, and Noël Kingsbury. 2008. *Planting Green Roofs and Living Walls.* Timber Press, Portland, Oregon.

Earth Pledge. 2005. *Green Roofs: Ecological Design and Construction.* Schiffer, Atglen, Pennsylvania.

Peck, Steven W. 2007. *Award-Winning Green Roof Designs.* Schiffer, Atglen, Pennsylvania.

Snodgrass, Edmund C., and Linda McIntyre. 2010. *The Green Roof Manual.* Timber Press, Portland, Oregon.

Snodgrass, Edmund C., and Lucie L. Snodgrass. 2006. *Green Roof Plants: A Resource and Planting Guide.* Timber Press, Portland, Oregon.

Weiler, Susan K., and Katrin Scholz-Barth. 2009. *Green Roof Systems: A Guide to the Planning, Design, and Construction of Landscapes over Structure.* John Wiley & Sons, Hoboken, New Jersey.

ACKNOWLEDGMENTS

WRITING THIS book has been, by necessity, a truly collaborative effort. It would not have been possible without the contribution of the designers and owners of all the individual projects, who have been extremely generous with their time, advice, and experiences. All are named along with their projects, but we as authors wish to record our sincere gratitude to all those involved with the projects that form the core of this book: we would not have been able to write the book without them.

We are particularly grateful to the following individuals and organizations who provided additional information and contacts for projects: Dan Cornwell of Green Estate Ltd, Sheffield, UK; Emilio Ancaya of Living Roofs, Inc., North Carolina, US; and Robyn Simcock of Landcare Research, New Zealand.

Many thanks also to Evangelia Bakratsa for the line drawings

We are indebted to the support, encouragement (and patience) of the Timber Press team: Anna Mumford in London for her unwavering enthusiasm for the book, Eve Goodman in Portland, and Lisa DiDonato Brousseau for her superb editing.

INDEX

ABOUT THE AUTHORS

MARTA HERRERO

NIGEL DUNNETT is a Reader in Urban Horticulture in the landscape department at the University of Sheffield, where he has developed innovative research programs on naturalistic and ecologically informed planting for gardens and public landscapes. He is director of The Green Roof Centre, Sheffield, and acts widely as a consultant on green roof design and planting, and sustainable garden and landscape design in general. He writes regularly for landscape and garden publications, including *Gardens Illustrated* and *The Garden*. With Noël Kingsbury he wrote *Planting Green Roofs and Living Walls*; with Andy Clayden, *Rain Gardens: Managing Water Sustainably in the Garden and Designed Landscape*.

DUSTY GEDGE is a green roof campaigner and founder of livingroofs.org, an independent green roofs association that promotes vegetated roof structures in urban and rural areas. With a background in community theatre, he is passionate about nature conservation and birdwatching. A frequent television and conference presenter on green roofs and biodiversity, he is particularly interested in teaching amateurs how to make green roofs. In 2004 he was awarded the Andrew Lees Memorial Award at the annual British Environment and Media Awards. He is currently president of the European Federation of Green Roof Associatons.

JANE SEBIRE

JOHN LITTLE is a partner in The Grass Roof Company, an award-winning, eco-friendly landscape design and management company that designs and builds green-roof buildings, designs and maintains school grounds and undertakes grounds maintenance work on behalf of local authorities. He has developed a broad reputation for his innovative green-roofed small buildings for schools, gardens and community use. His turf-roofed house won *Daily Telegraph* self-build house of the year in 1996.

GRAHAM SNODGRASS

EDMUND C. SNODGRASS started the first green roof nursery in the United States and has collaborated on green roof research with colleges and universities. A fifth-generation farmer and nurseryman, he is owner and president of Emory Knoll Farms Inc. and Green Roof Plants in Street, Maryland, specializing in plants and horticultural consulting for green roofs. He is coauthor, with Linda McIntyre, of *The Green Roof Manual: A Professional Guide to Design, Installation, and Maintenance*. He also wrote, with his wife, Lucie Snodgrass, *Green Roof Plants: A Resource and Planting Guide*.